NO                    TY
OF
PU          D1462280

# THE ORIGIN OF THE ICELANDERS

# THE ORIGIN OF
# THE ICELANDERS

By
BARTHI GUTHMUNDSSON

Translated with an introduction and notes by
LEE M. HOLLANDER

UNIVERSITY OF NEBRASKA PRESS · LINCOLN

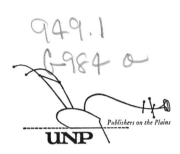

Publishers on the Plains

UNP

# Contents

Introduction by Lee M. Hollander        vii

## PART I
The Origin of the Icelanders        3

## PART II
The Origin of Skaldship in Iceland        21

   1. Skalds, Magic, Women's Rights        23

   2. Skalds, Swine, Saur- Farms        41

   3. Skalds, "Easterners," -AR Names        61

   4. Skalds, Sacrifices to Frey, Antiquities        83

   5. Skalds, Names, Genealogies        103

   6. Skalds, Ring Swords, Hildisvín        122

   7. The People of Iceland Are Older than the Settlement        146

Addenda        168

Index        169

# Introduction

It was in the summer of 1939 at the annual Congress of Scandinavists
in Copenhagen that the recently appointed Keeper of the National
Archives of Iceland, Barthi Guthmundsson, startled his learned col-
leagues with a paper on the nationality of the Icelanders. In it he sought
to prove with novel arguments that, contrary to the generally held
belief, important elements among the settlers were not of West
Scandinavian, i.e., Norwegian, but of East Scandinavian, Danish, and
ultimately Herulian, origin.

Here are some of his main points. The scant sources for the history of
the North during the Viking Age have made it clear that during the
first part of the ninth century there occurred a great expansion of
Danish power. Danish kings took possession of the coastal fringe of
Norway before invading northern France, England, and Ireland. The
conquest of Norway, which was split up into scores of mutually hostile
petty kingdoms, probably was easy, and Danish leaders naturally
acquired the holdings of native chiefs. But when Harald Fairhair,
toward the end of the century, consolidated Norway into one kingdom,
his most resolute opponents were the foreign, Danish overlords, who
had not yet been entirely assimilated to the Norwegian population.
After defeating them in the great Battle in the Hafrsfjord, Harald most
likely ousted them from their landed possessions. It was for this reason,
thinks Barthi, and not because Harald appropriated the alodial rights in
all Norway, that they fled, loading their household and retainers into
their ships, and sought security and lands in the newly discovered
island.

In subsequent articles Barthi exploited and broadened his new insight.

He soon perceived that it had implications greatly more far-reaching, chiefly, that the fugitives were not merely Norwegian emigrants but representatives of a culture other than that of Norway, as manifested from the very beginning of the new colony in thoroughgoing differences between it and the supposed motherland—differences which had baffled students of these matters for a long time.

Fundamentally, Iceland constituted itself as the first republic of post-Classic Europe, governed, not by kings or earls, as was Norway, but by assemblies of free men equal before the law. The leadership was, of course, in the hands of an upper class of large landowners, generally those who had fled from Norway. Each district had its *gothi*, vested with both temporal and sacerdotal authority—an institution peculiar to Iceland, but which seems to have existed also in Denmark. At the same time, no laws of primogeniture limited inheritance of land, as was the case in Norway.

In the sanctuaries erected and maintained by the *gothi* the worship of the fertility god Frey and his sister, Freya, predominated, at least in the first period of settlement, as it did in Sweden; whereas in Norway, Thor worship prevailed instead. The boar, symbol of fertility, was then the sacrificial animal of Iceland, and dear oaths were sworn on its bristles, with high-born women frequently officiating at the rites; as indeed the position of women was notably higher in Iceland than in Norway. This is specifically attested by the many metronymic names of persons and the remarkable percentage of farms bearing women's names, which again contrasts with conditions in Norway at the time.

Archaeologists attach much importance to the burial customs of a country or period as giving evidence of the beliefs held concerning the hereafter. Now, it had always been a matter of wonder why it is that in Iceland not a single burial mound from the Viking Age so far uncovered gives indication that cremation was ever practiced there, whereas in Norway during that time it was the rule. Nor can Christianity, with its belief in the resurrection of the body account for this, having been introduced only several generations after the Settlement. For Barthi this constitutes evidence that the leading class, here as everywhere initiating fashions, were not Norwegians. It is highly significant that except in Iceland interment was common at the time only in the Danish archipelago and in Jutland south of the Limfjord, which for Barthi is strong corroboration for his thesis that the leading families were of Danish and ultimately Herulian origin.

Still further, the antiquities so far unearthed in Icelandic burial mounds from Viking times, such as fibulae, chapes, and figurines, show unmistakable kinship in style with East Scandinavian artifacts, whether now they be heirlooms brought over or fabricated in Iceland. And most significantly: these were all unearthed at or near the farms of those settlers in whose families the skaldic art flourished, Frey worship persisted, traditions were preserved and handed down in the saga literature.

This brings us to the core of the matter and what must be considered the most important achievement of Barthi's detective and combinatory genius: He brings together and makes us perceive the vital connection between the facts observed and what constitutes Iceland's claim to imperishable fame in the annals of world literature, viz., that we owe to these fugitives of East Scandinavian extraction the foundation of a new state in which they could undisturbedly bring to fruition the culture they had inherited from their Danish-Herulian forebears—a culture activated originally by contact with the classical world.

I have here touched on what seem to me the chief aspects of Barthi's profoundly original work. After his untimely death in 1957 his friends Skúli Thortharson, who succeeded him, and Stefan Pjetursson, professor at the Reykjavík High School, collected and edited the eight articles here translated, together with nine others dealing with various aspects of Old Norse history and institutions, under the title *Uppruni Íslendinga* (The Origin of the Icelanders) (Reykjavík, 1959). The fact that these eight papers had for some reason appeared at various times between 1942 and 1951 in semipopular Icelandic journals hardly read

outside that country, together with the difficulty, even for Scandinavians, of Modern Icelandic no doubt accounts for the pioneering labors
of this great scholar remaining practically unknown, let alone being
accepted. The translation here offered aims to remedy this situation.

Had Barthi lived, he would no doubt have presented the subject in a
more condensed and rounded shape, with fewer repetitions such as are
evident, especially in the last paper. I have not felt called upon to alter
his work in any way or to weigh the merits of the arguments marshaled
by him. However, I did endeavor to furnish the documentation
demanded in rigorously scholarly writing, but which the editors
evidently failed to locate in his papers. I thank them for generous help
in this matter and for the translation of a number of neologisms, and
Mrs. Teresía Guthmundsson for the graciously given permission to
translate her husband's work.

LEE M. HOLLANDER

# PART I

# The Origin of the Icelanders

# The Origin of the Icelanders

So far as is known, it was Ari the Learned,[1] the son of Thorgils, who was the first to write about the settlement of Iceland. The beginning chapter of his *Íslendingabók* (Book of Icelanders) deals with this matter. Ari's account opens as follows: "Iceland was settled by Norwegians, to begin with, and during the life time of King Harald Fairhair, when Ívar Ragnarson had Saint Edmund, the king of England, put to death. That was 870 years after the birth of Christ, according to what we are told in his saga."[2] Following these words he tells of the coming to Iceland of the first settler, Ingólf Arnarson, and continues: "There was a great rush of people from Norway, until King Harald prohibited it because he feared that his land would be depopulated. Then they came to the agreement that every person who intended to sail from Norway to Iceland was to pay the king five ounces of silver, unless granted special dispensation."

In his brief account Ari does not state whether the settlers came from other lands than Norway. Nevertheless, one may gather from his wording that much points to a considerable participation in the colonization by people who were not of Norwegian origin: Ari mentions the four most important settlers—one in each Quarter—and remarks about three of them that they were of *norrœn* (Norse) origin. Clearly, this is not a random observation, because about the fourth of

[1] Ari Thorgilsson (1067–1148). His *Libellus Islendorum*, a pamphlet of eight parchment pages and eleven short chapters, is a résumé of Icelandic history, 870–1120. The following quotations are from Chapter I.
[2] I.e., The Life of St. Edmund (841–870), *Passio Sancti Eadmundi*, by Abbo of Fleury (Floriacensus), d. 1004.

3

these settlers, Ari says that he was a son of Earl Ragnvald of Mœr.[3] No
further explanation of his nationality was needed in his case. For that
matter Ari uses the designation *norrœn* in its more comprehensive
meaning, which may be best seen in his calling *norrœn* Helgi the Lean,
who was of Gautland (Gotland)[4] origin and brought up in the Western
Islands. It is, rather, between Norse and Celtic origin that Ari means to
draw a sharp line of demarcation. For this reason he states so carefully
what was the national origin of these four first settlers. This surprising
circumstance can hardly be explained except in one way: Ari was
aware that the admixture of Celtic blood had been of very considerable
extent in Iceland. Else it would not have occurred to him to mention
specifically about every single settler that he was of *norrœn* origin.

   Our chief source for the national origin of the Icelandic people is the
*Landnámabók* (the Book of Settlements).[5] The main portion of it was
first written in the early part of the twelfth century. In this book we are
told about a little more than four hundred settlers, and concerning a
great many of them, whence they came. And from the accounts there
given about them one can gather that the great majority came directly
from Norway, more particularly from the western shires of that land.
At the same time it is clear that a great number of people moved to
Iceland "from west over the sea"; and among those who came from
the British Islands many evidently were Celts. In the Book of Settlements more than ten Celtic settlers are mentioned, but this number of
course gives little idea of the admixture of Celtic blood in Iceland. One
must suppose that many Celtic servants followed the Norse colonizers.
Besides, some of them were half-breeds or were married to Celtic
women. Eloquent witnesses of the Celtic participation in the original
settlement of Iceland are the names of persons such as Bekan, Bjólan,

   [3] The present (North and South) Mœre, central west provinces of Norway.
   [4] The present (East and West) Götland, provinces of central Sweden.
   [5] *Landnámabók Íslands (Ldn.)*, compiled *ca.* 1200, and extant in three main manu-
scripts. More than four thousand persons and about fourteen hundred place names
are mentioned in it. The best edition is that by Finnur Jónsson, 1925. Consult the
excellent index for names of persons, places, clans, etc.

Bjollok, Dufgus, Dufthak, Gilli, Grelǫth, Kjallak, Kjaran, Kjartan, Kormák, Kalman, Kylan, Konal, Melkorka, Mobil, Myrun, and Njál, all known from our old history.

Unfortunately the authors of the Book of Settlements only very rarely tell us about the national origin of the Norse immigrants. Two of them are in so many words called Swedish, and three times the word *norræn* is used about settlers. One is said to have been Gautish on his father's side, and Flemish on his mother's. Finally, one land-taker bears the surname of "the Dane," which surname of course owes its origin to the fact that the colonist in question had been reared in Denmark. He is called the son of Garthar, the son of Svavar, who was the first Norse man to discover Iceland.[6] About Garthar it is stated that he was the son of Svavar the Swede, and that he had possessions on the Danish island of Seeland. According to the Book of Settlements Garthar was on his way to the Hebrides in order to fetch the paternal inheritance of his wife, when he was driven northward out of his course and discovered Iceland. In case this tradition is correct it would give us some hint that in the ninth century the Norwegians were not the only ones to sail the Atlantic north of the British Islands.[7]

The doctrine that the Icelanders are of Norwegian origin is centuries old. It seems to appear first even in the writings of Icelandic historians of the thirteenth century. Nor is it difficult to explain how this belief arose. Statements made by the authors of the Book of Settlements in the first part of the twelfth century imply again and again that the great majority of settlers were of Norwegian stock. But since the Icelandic historians of the thirteenth and fourteenth centuries had no accurate idea of the historical conditions of the ninth century, it was to be expected that they took these accounts to be trustworthy testimony about the Norwegian origin of their nation. It is hardly to be expected that they realized that, even though the settlers hailed from Norway, this was no proof of their Norwegian origin. But we now know that

[6] *Ldn.* § 3.
[7] *Ldn.* § 4 also mentions the Norwegian Nadodd as having discovered Iceland.

at the time Iceland was colonized, Danish and Swedish colonies were
scattered far and wide over the face of Europe. So before the conclusion
is drawn from the statements of the Book of Settlements that the
Icelanders are the descendants of the Norwegians we need to establish
for sure whether the Norwegians were masters in their own land
during the generations immediately preceding the occupation of Iceland. This has not been done; nor is it likely that we shall ever be able
to do so.

We learn that most settlers in Iceland were the descendants of Norwegian freeholders of chieftainly kin. However, there is no proof that
alodial laws ever were adopted in Iceland in the olden times. The word
*óðal* (alodial patrimony, land held as absolute property) does not occur
once in our ancient laws. And there is hardly one example, in the early
literature of Iceland, of landed property there being called *óðal*. For that
matter, it is unlikely that Icelanders were altogether unacquainted with
the ancient customs so firmly rooted among the Norwegians. One may
say, to be sure, that parcels of landed property needed to have gone for
some longer time from father to son in the same family before they,
according to Norwegian custom and law, could be called alodial
possessions. But considering that a great number of Icelandic manorial
estates were half a century old when the code of laws for the whole
country was established, this has little to say, because according to
ancient Norwegian law[8] one could obtain absolute possession of lands
even in a shorter space of time. So it cannot be said that there is much
probability of the Icelandic settlers having been brought up in the
knowledge of alodial law and Norwegian class statutes. Nor does it
change matters if, as is acknowledged generally, Bugge's opinion[9]
holds, viz., that alodial law prevailed of old in the new Norwegian
colonies on the Orkneys and the Shetland Islands. With all this in mind
it is difficult to make these facts agree with the view that the chieftainly
class of saga times was derived from Norwegian freeholders.

[8] *Gulathings Law* § 270.
[9] Alexander Bugge, *Norges Historie* (Kristiania, 1910), p. 102.

In contradistinction to what was the case among Norwegians in the olden times, all freeborn Icelanders were equal before the law, enjoying one and all the same legal rights. All the same, from the very beginning there obtained great class distinctions. The highborn families and the class of *gothar* lorded it over the common farmers. It was they who appear actually to have had the say about everything. The *gothi* was both the spiritual leader of the people as temple priest and their overlord in temporal matters. It was with the position of power of this class as given that the ancient constitution of Iceland was primarily established. Our sources lend no support to the view that any such class ever existed in Norway. One can, on the contrary, draw the conclusion from their existence in Iceland that the Icelanders did not pattern their constitution after a Norwegian model. We possess a considerable number of contemporary sources which preserve the history of the Norwegians during the Viking Period, such as Skaldic verse. To be sure, this deals chiefly with the wars and conquests of their kings, still there is likewise frequent reference to the social classes of Norwegian society as well as to the struggles between heathendom and Christianity. Nevertheless there is no mention whatever of a *gothi*. And in the traditions as revealed in the writings of the old Icelandic saga authors the same holds true: not once in the copious accounts of the missions in Norway and the struggle there against heathenism is there any mention of *gothar*. It is almost surprising that the Icelandic historians, owing to influence from their own history, never in their accounts give Norwegian chieftains of ancient times the title of *gothi*. In this case, then, we are bound to draw our conclusions from their silence: the Icelandic rule of the *gothar* as a social phenomenon definitely is not an inheritance from Norwegian social institutions.

No one is likely to doubt that both the alodial law and the rule of the *gothar* are much older among the Scandinavian peoples than the colonization of Iceland. If the Icelanders were mainly of Norwegian stock one should think that these institutions, so fundamental in the social structure of either land, would be common for Norwegians and

Icelanders, at least during the heathen period. Instead, it is clear that we are here dealing with wholly different national characteristics, both as to cultural and social conditions, characteristics so significant that they unquestionably point to the circumstance that those of our ancestors who at the start had most to do with establishing this kind of government in our land were, generally speaking, not Norwegians at all though they hailed from Norway.

In conformity with the accounts of the Book of Settlements historians have always maintained that the bulk of the colonists came from the western shires of Norway. Philologists have even believed they could prove this by comparing the development of Icelandic speech with that of the West Norwegian dialects.[10] But archaeologists also have a say in this matter. They have investigated a great number of graves in the western districts of Norway which date from the Viking Age, and have come to the definite conclusion that cremation still was of great importance there during that period, that graves showing incineration constitute the great majority. In Iceland, too, a considerable number of tombs from the Viking Age and in various parts of the country have been discovered and investigated. Among them there is not a single one showing cremation. Nor is there anywhere in the rich ancient literature of Iceland mention made of cremation as a religious rite for Icelanders, for which reason the archaeologists take it as an established fact that cremation was not practiced by either the original settlers or their descendants.

For this strange state of affairs a satisfactory explanation has so far not been given. And none is to be expected as long as one puts faith in the time-honored doctrine of the Norwegian origin of the Icelandic people. But once we free ourselves of the article of faith that the Icelanders are in the main of West Norwegian stock the answer is clear: the radically different burial customs of Norwegian emigrants in the Viking Age are likely to be rooted primarily in the customs of immigrants foreign to

[10] Most recently, K. G. Chapman in his monograph *Icelandic-Norwegian Linguistic Relationships* (Oslo, 1962).

Norway, i.e., of people who had abandoned the old custom of cremation. These immigrants tended to cling to the culture and habits of their
forefathers—of course because they had settled in the new land (in this
case Norway) as conquerors and overlords of the people of that land.
They buried their dead after the fashion of their old home, even though
the native Norwegians on their part perpetuated the ancient customs of
emigrants of their nation.

Now we can understand why such momentous differences obtained
between the customs of Norwegians and those of the Icelanders in
heathen times: the great bulk of those who emigrated to Iceland from
Norway were descended from people who were foreigners in Norway.
And just as in Norway their ancestors had held in honor the customs
and ways of their native land, their descendants in Iceland did likewise;
and it is for this reason that cremation is something unknown among
the heathen Icelanders.

It is clear why precisely the people who had not taken up cremation
made their way to Iceland: at the very time Iceland was being settled
a large-scale revolution took place in Norway; the foundations were
being laid there of a national kingdom. The very numerous petty
kingdoms were welded into one kingdom. And the foreign immigrants
who had ruled over the native population for some time either had to
accommodate themselves to Norwegian laws and customs or else
remove themselves. Many of them chose the alternative of seeking
refuge in the newly discovered land to the west in the Atlantic. There
they founded a dominion of their own in the fashion which suited them
best.

To what ancestry, then, do these first standard-bearers of Old
Icelandic culture trace their origin? It is the burial places of the Viking
Age of a thousand years ago, those silent witnesses, which guide us to
the solution of this problem. The archaeologists have demonstrated
that cremation was in vogue in practically all of Scandinavia during
the generation immediately preceding the colonization of Iceland,
except in the Danish islands and in Jutland south of the Limfjord.

Thus one of the main institutions of the Icelandic people appears to have grown up in the heart of the old Danish kingdom. By Danish emigrants Danish religious ideas and funeral rites were imported to Norway, and subsequently from there to Iceland by the descendants of this people: as said, no burial places showing traces of cremation have been found in either Iceland or the Danish islands, which fact rather clearly points to where the origin of the Icelanders is to be sought.

Let us return to the important differences which our sources of information show to have prevailed between the way of life of the Icelanders and that of the Norwegians during the Viking Age. They cannot possibly be explained to any satisfaction on the premise that Iceland was a Norwegian colony. From a sociological point of view it is altogether without a foundation to talk about the *gothar*, the upper class of the Icelandic people, as heirs of the *hersar*[11] in Norway. For that matter, this view is likely to have few if any spokesmen among scholars. But it is equally unlikely that the rule of the *gothar*, so characteristic for Iceland, had no prototype among the forefathers of the Icelanders. Again, the thousand-year-old testimony is heard from: Danish runic monuments of the Viking Period found in the Danish islands give clear evidence that *gothar* as a class of chieftains existed in Denmark at the time Iceland was occupied, and precisely there where no burial places of the ninth century showing cremation are found. To repeat, it is only among Icelanders and Danes that we know for certain that the institution of *gothar* existed.

On the other hand, in neither of the two countries did any alodial law prevail, but rather a remarkable equality of rights between the various social classes. Here, then, certainly there is a salient and characteristic social organization common to both Icelanders and Danes of old to which there is nothing comparable among the Norwegians. When due attention is paid to the fact that, during the first centuries after the settlement, intercourse between Icelanders and Norwegians was ever so much livelier than between Icelanders and Danes, it is clear

[11] *Hersir* (pl. *hersar*): chieftain, leader of a *herath* (district).

that it will not do to shrug off and pass over in silence what has been emphasized above.

It is hardly necessary to remind the reader that in the olden times the Icelanders called their mother tongue, the speech common to all the lands of the North, *dǫnsk tunga* (the Danish Tongue). In our sources this designation is encountered for the first time in the verse of Sigvat Thórtharson[12] early in the eleventh century, and later on we find it here and there during the next three and a half centuries. Only in the thirteenth century does the designation *norrœn* (Norse) begin to gain ground in Icelandic, due, no doubt, to Norwegian influence. There is no doubt whatever about the Danish Tongue in the sense of "our language" being the original name among native Icelanders for the language they spoke. That is most clearly seen in the language of the law. There, only the expressions "the Danish Tongue" or "our speech" are used about the Old Norse language. To be sure, the laws of Iceland were not committed to writing until 1118,[13] but that is of no importance in this connection. It is evident that the designation "the Danish Tongue" of the language Icelanders spoke and wrote was not borrowed from the Danes after the colonization was concluded. Nor is there any likelihood that Norwegians used that designation to signify the Old Norse speech.

Just why was it, then, that the settlers called their language Danish? To this there never has been given a satisfactory answer. The same is true about this weighty matter as about Icelandic burial customs in the Viking Age and about the *gothar*, who did not adopt the alodial law in their country, though they had the right to claim chieftainly descent. All these matters have been discussed much, but it is safe to say that little has been accomplished to explain them. The inveterate idea that the Icelandic people is almost exclusively of Norwegian origin has obstructed the view. And yet the explanation of all these problems lies close at hand, and in a word is this: It was people of Danish origin who

12 In his poem *Víkinga Vísur*, stanza 15.
13 In the so-called *Grágás*.

at first had the greatest part in pointing the way in the development of the national life of the Icelanders.

Now it so happens that a very trustworthy source of information, viz., the *Annals of Einhard*,[14] puts the matter beyond doubt, to wit, that in the beginning of the ninth century the Danes expanded their power north of the Skagerak. We learn that in the year 813 the Danish kings Harald and Ragnfröth were not in their homelands but in the Norwegian shire of West Fold[15] with their army to put down the revolt which the chieftains and inhabitants there had made against their rule. Concerning the location of West Fold, it is clearly stated that it was "the most distant part" of the Danish dominion, and opposite the northernmost point of Britain. There cannot be any mistake about the writer of these annals using the term West Fold not only for that part of Norway which now bears that name, but also for the contiguous shire of Agthir. This is not surprising, since various circumstances suggest that in those days West Fold was predominant in southeast Norway. It may also be taken for granted that the Danish kings in that period extended their rule over all the coast lands north of the Skagerak and, in fact, had a wide sway there.

After the Danish kings had returned home after putting down the rebellion in southern Norway, they in their turn were forced to flee their own land in haste before the sons of that great warrior king of the Danes, Guthröth, who had died three years before. Thereupon Hárek, one of the sons of Guthröth, was king of Denmark for almost forty years. There is no support in our sources for thinking that the rule of the Danes north of the Skagerak had weakened during that time. On the contrary, there are excellent reasons for assuming that they extended their sway and obtained dominion over the inner passages north along the west coast of Norway by taking up their abode where most convenient for that purpose. We know that in those times the Danes

[14] Erroneously so called and supposedly written by Einhard (770–840), the adviser and biographer of Charlemagne. *Sub anno* 813.

[15] (West and East) Fold, the former name of the lands surrounding the Oslofjord.

launched large-scale attacks against the old civilized countries of western Europe. They harried far and wide about the great Frankish empire and all the way south to the Mediterranean, whilst at the same time descending in force on northern Germany and the British islands.[16] In the years when the colonization of Iceland took its beginning, the Danes had subjugated a large part of England and had made permanent settlements in both Ireland and the coast lands of continental western Europe. Everywhere we see the Viking hosts following the trade routes and attempting to take by force those towns where there was most expectation of booty. Considering this, it appears altogether inconceivable that they would have disdained to dominate the inner passages of the Norwegian coast north to the dried fish and fur markets of northern Norway. And it appears equally certain that the motley and thinly populated petty Norwegian kingdoms had not been able to ward off the encroachments and attacks of the Danes, any more than West Fold, which, as we know for certain, the Danish kings were beginning to subjugate at the beginning of the Viking Age.

In his Annals,[17] Bishop Prudentius of Troyes relates that in the year 850 war broke out between King Hárek, the son of Guthröth, and two of his nephews. The king was forced to cede to them parts of his realm. At the same time this happened we learn from Irish sources[18] that a fierce internecine struggle arose between the Scandinavian vikings in Ireland. The two parties warring against each other were called *Daunitar* and *Lochlannar*. After three years of fighting the *Daunitar* got the upper hand. In the year 853 Óláf,[19] the son of King Guthröth Rognvaldsson, arrived in Ireland with the mission of his father to collect the tribute from the Irish; and to his banner flocked *Daunitar* as well as *Lochlannar*.

[16] For a recent work on the subject, see S. H. Sawyer, *The Age of Vikings* (1962).

[17] *Annales Bertiniani, sub anno* 850.

[18] *Annals of Ireland: Three Fragments*, ed. John O'Donovan (Dublin, 1860), pp. 115 ff.

[19] I.e., Óláf the White. He ruled 853–871.

Now it seems evident that the *Lochlannar* were the subjects of King Guthröth Rognvaldsson. Strangely, the *Daunitar*, who had just overcome the *Lochlannar* after a deadly struggle, became the followers of his son Óláf without offering him the least resistance. The most plausible explanation of this is the one given by Zimmer,[20] viz., that both *Daunitar* and *Lochlannar* were Danes. If such was the case, then it is easy to understand why the former were reconciled to the leadership of the King's son from *Lochlann*. As soon as peace was established in the homeland the vikings in Ireland also stopped fighting one another. Schück maintained,[21] for good reasons, that Guthröth, king of *Lochlann* was no other than one of the nephews of the King Hárek mentioned by Prudentius.

This Óláf, the son of Guthröth, ruled in Dublin for eighteen years and is of great importance in the history of Ireland. He is one of the few viking kings of the ninth century who are mentioned also in Icelandic sources. Ari the Learned called himself a direct descendant of Óláf on the sword side.[22] He makes Óláf a scion of the Swedish Yngling kings who ruled in Uppsala, but knows nothing about King Guthröth Rognvaldsson, his father, stating King Óláf to be the son of Ingjald. Now it is strange that, conflicting with the information given by Ari concerning King Óláf's kin, there persisted, precisely in the district from which Ari hailed, a tradition that this Óláf was of the Danish royal race. Although such traditions by themselves may not be of much value as proof that both King Guthröth and Óláf in Dublin were Danish, yet they unquestionably support the presumption which can be deduced from foreign sources of information concerning their close relationship to the Danish king Hárek Guthrötharson.

We may take it for certain that the dominion of King Guthröth Rognvaldsson lay north of the Skagerak. And we can hardly doubt that by the designation *Lochlann* Norway is meant, or at least part of that

[20] *Zeitschrift für deutsches Altertum*, XXXV (1891), 131 ff.
[21] *Historisk tidskrift* (Stockholm, 1895), pp. 73 ff.
[22] See his *Íslendingabók*, Appendix III.

country. Finds of objects dating from the Viking Age undoubtedly point up the fact that connections and intercourse between Ireland and Scotland, on the one hand, and Norway on the other, were much closer then than those with the other Scandinavian countries; but this does not necessarily mean that it was principally Norwegians who founded the viking kingdoms in Ireland and harried in Scotland during the ninth century. Rather, it supports the view that the power of King Guthröth was backed by Danish immigrants to that country.

Although the sources for the history of Scandinavia during the ninth century are very meager, yet one can make out from them that the sway of the Danes north of the Skagerak is likely to have lasted until Norway, late in that century, became a united kingdom under Harald Fairhair. According to the statement of an ancient Irish source[23] King Guthröth Rognvaldsson of *Lochlann* in 871 sent a message to his son Óláf in Dublin to return home to assist him in putting down a rebellion which had broken out against him. And according to the chronology of Ari the Learned the Battle in the Hafrsfjord must have occurred exactly at that time, either 871 or 872. Gustav Storm has adduced convincing arguments[24] that (among others) King Guthröth Rognvaldsson and his son Óláf were opponents of Harald Fairhair in that conflict. If this is the case, which is most probable, then the Battle in the Hafrsfjord marks the end of Danish rule in Norway for a considerable time. The memory of the lost dominion of the Danes in Norway was kept alive by the Danish kings. King Harald Gormsson made claim to overlordship in Norway and succeeded in subduing it. Likewise his son, Svein Forkbeard, and his grandson, Canute the Powerful. So there is no cause for wonder if during the first part of the ninth century Danish military might was able to overcome the petty Norwegian kingdoms, before the foundations of a political unification were laid to make Norway a national kingdom. One could almost say that things were bound to happen that way.

[23] See note 18, above.
[24] *Norsk Historisk Tidsskrift*, anden række, II (1880), 313th ff.

Of contemporary Norwegian sources of information about King Harald Fairhair there exist now only two fragmentary lays by Thorbjorn hornklofi,[25] the *Glymdrápa* (War Alarum *drápa* or lay) and the *Haraldskvæthi* (Lay of Harald). From the latter poem we get a fairly clear idea that some popular opposition and pride against Danish dominion prevailed in Norway in the latter part of the ninth century. Yet the poet himself seems to set the Danes a degree higher than the Norwegians. This is explicable only by the premise of the former overlordship and influence of the Danes in Norway. There can be no mistake about that. Hornklofi expressly makes it redound to the praise of his king that he had taken a Danish consort, rejecting his Norwegian mistresses:

> The high-born liege-lord
> wed the lady from Denmark—
> broke with his Rogaland sweethearts
> and their sisters from Horthaland,
> with those from Heithmork
> and Hálogaland also.[26]

The thought behind encomiums like this might well suggest that at the time Hornklofi recited his poem King Harald did not regard himself as a Norwegian. This would agree remarkably with the skald Thjóthólf (ór Hvini)[27] in his *Ynglingatal* (Enumeration of the Ynglings), calling King Eystein of West Fold, an ancestor of Harald, "the Gautish prince."[28]

In his poem Hornklofi calls King Harald both "the King of the Norwegians" and "the sovereign of the Eastmen." The latter appellation reminds one involuntarily of the statement in the *Historia Norvegiæ*[29] that the District of Throndheim had been settled by

[25] Norwegian skald of the ninth century.

[26] *Haraldskvæthi*, stanza 14.

[27] Norwegian skald who flourished *ca.* 900.

[28] *Ynglingatal*, stanza 31.

[29] Anonymous Latin work written during the first part of the thirteenth century.

Swedes. Here we probably have to deal with a Throndheim tradition which must have had its origin in there having at one time been an important influx of Swedes to the district.When this took place may be inferred from finds in northern Norway dating from the very beginning of the Viking Age. Shetelig[30] has called attention to the fact that antiquities of northern Norway from that time bear such unmistakable witness to Swedish cultural influence that we may assume a considerable influx from Sweden (in those districts), possibly involving great numbers of Swedes who with the right of the stronger took up their abode among Norwegians in northern Norway. Before the start of the great viking expeditions to the lands east of the Baltic and to Russia, the need of the Swedish people to expand seems to have found an outlet westward to northern Norway, and most likely also to the Uppland Districts.[31]

If, then, much points to the establishment of Swedes in Norway north of the mountains in the century before the colonization of Iceland, one may assume that the participation of people of Swedish origin in it was considerable. Both the system of naming and statements in the Book of Settlements would seem to support this supposition. Also, it is important to observe that of the thirty-nine settlers who are there called the most notable, about a third came from the northern districts of Norway.With one exception, they established themselves in the southern and eastern quarter of Iceland. More particularly, those from northern Norway appear to have settled in the eastern fjords. Most of them were from the Throndheim districts, but some also from Vors in Horthaland; and much points to people of Swedish origin having settled at Vors some time before the colonization of Iceland. In this connection we may call attention to the kin of Hortha-Kari and Thorvith, the son of Freyvith. To the former family belongs Úlfljót, the first lawspeaker of Iceland.

As is well known, the ancient Icelandic historians have offered as an

[30] *Det norske folks liv og historie gjennem tidene* (Oslo, 1930), pp. 157 f.
[31] I.e., of Norway.

explanation of the emigration from Norway to Iceland that King
Harald had deprived the farmers of their alodial rights and had taken
possession of all their lands. "The larger farmers and chieftains fled their
land to avoid such oppression and injustice, at least those who did not
want to become tenants of the king."[32] Thus the remarkable explanation given as the main reason of Iceland's having been settled by
Norwegians. Now it is quite certain that the Icelandic historians of the
thirteenth century knew very well that the alodial law prevailed in
Norway and had done so from time immemorial. It is for this reason
that Snorri Sturluson relates that King Hákon the Good, the foster son
of King Æthelstán of England, restored the alodial rights of the
Norwegian farmers and handed them back their old possessions.[33] In
this manner Snorri attempts to vindicate the doctrine that the settlers of
Iceland had fled Norway for the reason that they did not want to be
tenants of King Harald. So we can see that it was not by chance that
Snorri thinks it was Hákon who returned to the farmers the right to
their landed possessions. He was proclaimed king just at the time when
the settlement of Iceland was completed, and he was considered the
greatest lawgiver.

One may regard it as self-evident that the old belief of King Harald's
having deprived his subjects of their landed possessions is incorrect. If
he had attempted to carry out such violent measures against the upper
classes of the country, his royal power would have come to a sudden
end. Also, the greatest scholars have demonstrated that the old statements about the governmental measures of Harald Fairhair have not
stood the test of scientific criticism, least of all the accounts of his
seizing the alodial possessions. At the same time, when considering the
matter in this light, the question arises how the ancient historians con-
ceived their explanation of the emigration from Norway to Iceland,
which conflicts so strongly with the well-known fact that the alodial
law prevailed in Norway (in their time), and had prevailed there since

[32] The quotation is from *Egils saga*, Chapter 4.
[33] *Heimskringla, Hákonar saga gotha*, Chapter 1.

time immemorial. It is easy to answer that question. Evidently there were stories current among the chieftainly families of Iceland that their progenitors who removed themselves to Iceland during the rule of Harald Fairhair had done so because they were deprived of their landed possessions. After King Harald, with the assistance of the native landed proprietors, had succeeded in uniting Norway, those foreigners who had settled on the land were forced to give up the alodial possessions which they had seized. Those families who had sojourned in Norway for the shortest time were, of course, hardest hit. And now we understand why the colonists came mainly from the western districts of Norway and from Hálogaland: There these foreigners had settled later than in the Throndheim districts and the southeast portions of Norway, and therefore were least inclined to accommodate themselves to the governmental and cultural ways of the Norwegians when Harald Fairhair rose to power as king of the whole Norwegian people.

Now, although the main cause for the great outflow of people from Norway is likely to have been the one outlined above, naturally it was not only people of Danish and Swedish descent who emigrated to Iceland. Doubtless a considerable number of Norwegians went along. Additionally we must assume that very many of the colonists were of Dano-Norwegian or Swedish-Norwegian stock. But of this we may be sure that, as set forth above, Danish influence was pre-eminent in the early development of the national life of the Icelanders. That does not mean, of course, that people of Danish descent constituted the majority of the inhabitants of Iceland at the conclusion of the century during which settlement took place. Also, it must not be forgotten, when discussing the nationality of the Icelanders, that the words of Ari unmistakably indicate that a blending of Celtic and Norse stock prevailed more importantly in our country than is generally acknowledged.

## PART II

# The Origin of Skaldship in Iceland

# 1. Skalds, Magic, Women's Rights

Although the Norwegians and the Icelanders are closely related peoples, yet there are incredible differences in their ancient cultures. In certain respects both peoples show clearer marks of relationship now than nine centuries ago. The difference between their cultures in the olden times becomes apparent when we consider their main aspects. From the very beginning differences manifest themselves in the constitutions of the two countries, the stratification of society, and the legal rights of the individual. The difference between the burial customs of the Norwegians and those of the Icelanders in heathen times eliminates any doubt that the religious ideas of people here were shaped by other cultural conditions than were those of their cousins to the east. And beginning from the earliest times the Icelanders became foremost among Scandinavians in the realm of skaldship. It would seem that this wordcraft, together with the culture that bred it, almost vanished in Norway, following those emigrants who colonized Iceland. The time does appear ripe to investigate the causes for this mysterious and most remarkable phenomenon in (our) literary history.

From the conclusion of the settlement of Iceland on, nearly all the court poets of the kings of Norway were Icelanders. This is well known and indisputable. In his large History of Old Norse Literature,[1] Finnur Jónsson enumerates the Icelandic court poets now known to us. From the tenth and eleventh centuries he gives the names of forty-nine court poets. We know enough about thirty-five of them to be fairly sure about the ancestral home and birthplace of each of them. Now, it is

[1] *Den oldnorske og oldislandske Litteraturs Historie* (Copenhagen, 1920–1924), Vol. I, § 7.

curious that there is no court poet known from the Eastern Quarter of Iceland. Calling to mind the rarity of skalds among the related people of Norway in ancient times, our attention unconsciously turns to the Quarter of our land which produced no court poets. This may furnish us a hint as to how to proceed in our investigation. It is clear that skald-ship had not in ancient times struck deep roots either in the eastern part of our land or in the Thingeyjar District. East of the Eyjafjord and of the Markarfljót River there is only one court skald among the thirty-five: Glúm Geirason was brought up in the neighborhood of Lake Mývatn, but while still young moved west, where his family settled in the Breithafjord District.

We may well divide our ancient skalds into two groups, court skalds and poets of occasional verse. After enumerating the latter group from three Quarters, Finnur Jónsson expresses himself about as follows:[2] "It is strange how few skalds are known from the eastern part of our land. There is hardly one we can mention except Grím Droplaugarson." Yet he took account of all skalds in his list of poets. In addition to Grím, he mentions two skalds from the Múlathing District, Helgi Ásbjarnarson, to whom is ascribed one stanza, and one Thorkel Svartaskáld (Swart Poet), who is grouped with skalds only on account of his surname.

From the Northern Quarter east of the Eyjafjord, three skalds are mentioned besides Glúm Geirason, and two in the Skaptafell District. Among these skalds is Vǫthu-Brand of Laxamýr, who is said to have capped verses with another man and to have bested him. All these are called skalds for the same reason as is Helgi Ásbjarnarson: Their names are in the old texts, each mentioned as being the author of one occa-sional stanza. As was to be expected, Finnur Jónsson wondered about the paucity of skalds in the Eastern Quarter and the general lack of lays there. He had counted altogether about 120 skalds in the tenth and eleventh centuries whose domicile it was easy to ascertain rather definitely. Only nine of them belonged to the country east of the Eyja-fjord and the Markarfljót River. And only one among them, Glúm

[2] *Op. cit.*, p. 519.

Geirason, was of any distinction. But he might as well be counted among the Westfjord skalds, as most likely he learned his craft in the Breithafjord country.

From Bishop Gissur Ísleifsson's[3] list of farmers liable to the tax one may obtain a fairly clear idea about the proportional number of persons in the four Quarters during the first centuries of the colonization of Iceland. About the turn of the twelfth century there were seven hundred taxable farmers in the East Quarter, twelve hundred in the North Quarter, nine hundred in the West Quarter, and one thousand in the South Quarter. When the Thingeyjar and Eyjafjalla Districts are added to the East Quarter of the ancient times, it is clear that this portion of the country by no means had fewer people than each of the others, at least significantly fewer. There is little likelihood of our arriving more closely at the exact number of inhabitants than to reckon all four Quarters about even in numbers in ancient times, because each had from nine to ten hundred taxable farmers.

I shall now in this section call the old Vestfirthinga Quarter, bounded by the Hvítá River in the Borgarfjord District and the Hrútafjartharā River, Westland; the old Northlendinga Quarter west of the Eyjafjord and the Vathla Heath, Northland; the old Sunnlendinga Quarter west of the Markarfljót River, Southland; but all of the tract east of the Eyjafjord and the Markarfljót River, Eastland, so that the Eastland would extend to the landtake of Helgi the Lean on Kristness and that of Ketil hæng up to Hof.

Using Finnur Jónsson's list of skalds in ancient times, they would be apportioned as follows:

Westland: 13 court poets and 33 occasional poets—total, 46
Northland: 13 court poets, 28 occasional poets—total, 41
Southland: 8 court poets, 15 occasional poets—total, 23
Eastland: 1 court poet, 8 occasional poets—total, 9

These figures speak a clear language: Measured by the numbers of

[3] 1042–1118. *Kristni saga*, Chapter 16. Also Ari, *Íslendingabók*, Chapter 3.

inhabitants, Eastland has three to four times fewer skalds than could be expected, and Westland, fully five times more skalds than Eastland. In this comparision it is, of course, necessary to keep in mind the disparate amount of source material available for each part of the country. Nevertheless, it will be immediately evident that the premises built on this foundation are by themselves insufficient to explain the facts. We observe at once that the difference in the number of skalds belonging to the different parts of the country is by far more telling with regard to the court poets than with the occasional skalds. And yet we might expect that the memory of the court poets would have been preserved rather evenly, whatever their origin. First and foremost it was their lays about the kings which kept their names alive. Too, it is a well-known fact that, down to recent times, the West and the North of our country have greatly excelled the South and the East in poetic production and other literary activity. Most important, though, is the fact that the sagas themselves indicate that in the eastern part of our country in the ancient times people rarely composed poetry, and poorly preserved such as had been composed. There is not one stanza in the Ljósvetninga saga, only one in the Reykdœla saga, and that by the skald Víga-Glúm, who hailed from the Eyjafjord District. The latter exception is worth noting, because we may infer from it that the author of this saga scarcely would have passed by such stanzas as preserved the matter of his saga if they had existed and were known to him. The Vápnfjord sagas, like the Ljósvetninga saga, contain no verse whatever; and the same is true of the sagas of Thorstein Síthu-Hallsson, of Hrafnkel Freysgothi, and of the *thættir* (short stories) dealing with happenings in Eastland. Stanzas are found only in the Droplaugarsona saga and in the account of the slaying of Thorstein Síthu-Hallsson. Altogether, there are ten stanzas preserved in the Eastland sagas, and three of these are *draumvísur* (dream stanzas). This output of verse constitutes a thirteenth part of the stanzas of the Egils saga alone. It is not necessary to expatiate on the abundance of stanzas in the sagas of the West and Northland, but it is worth while calling attention to how many of these sagas concern events in the lives of the best skalds; thus, the Egils saga, the Gunnlaugs saga, the Bjarnar saga (Hitdœlakappa), the Gísla saga, the Hávarthar saga, the Fóstbrœthra saga, the Kormáks saga, the Grettis saga, the Hallfrethar saga, and the Víga-Glúms saga. Among the sagas of the Eastland there is no parallel to this, unless indeed it is permissible in this connection to mention the Droplaugarsona saga.

It is evident that during the first centuries of the history of Iceland there existed a considerable difference in cultural conditions between the western and the eastern halves of our country. This is a fact which cannot be called in question. The number of skalds alone bears that out sufficiently. From this, one may conclude that in the beginning those families that practiced the art of skaldship for the most part had chosen their habitation in the West and Northland, more especially in the Vathlathing District, including the Fljót District, in the Húnavatns-thing District, the Ísafjarthardjúp, the Breithafjord settlements, about Snæfellsness, and on the south side of the Vestfirthinga Quarter. Nor do we have to search far to find clear and distinctive features of the parti-cular culture of those families which laid stress on skaldship. In Finnur Jónsson's enumeration of skalds of the tenth and eleventh centuries more than a hundred skalds are named after their father or mother. Ten of them are in the ancient sources named after their mother. Now, even if this group were fewer by half than is the case, yet we might consider this most remarkable: the men's names known from the times mentioned probably number some thousands, but I have not succeeded in finding among them more than twenty-five named after their mother. In other words, with the exception of a skald and his brothers and sisters, it is most unusual that more than one, or possibly two, of a hundred persons are thus easily recognizable as to name; whereas with the skalds this is the case with nearly every tenth person. This strange characteristic of skald families is so pronounced, so far removed from the possibility of mere chance, that I haven't gone to the trouble to count and classify the multitude of names of persons that occur in the ancient sources. Still, to be on the safe side I consulted Bogi Melsteth's survey of Icelandic shipowners and merchants in saga times[4] to compare with the number of skalds; and I found there that, excluding the skalds and their brothers and sisters, nearly two hundred persons are named after their fathers, but only one after his mother, viz., Sigurth Gunnhildarson, who figures in the Harthar saga.

Too, it is worth noting that this custom of metronymy prevails far more among the court skalds than among the occasional poets. Among the court skalds, every sixth one is named after his mother, but among the occasional poets, every fourteenth or fifteenth. This is quite natural. On the whole, the list of court poets is by far the more reliable; whereas among the occasional poets there are several of whom one is not sure whether they bear by rights the designation of skald, while on the other hand, one may consider most court skalds as ranking among the first-class ones and belonging to those families that conferred most distinction on Old Icelandic poetic culture. For this reason I shall now turn my attention more particularly to this group of skalds.

Now to mention those court skalds who are named after their mother. They are: Eilíf Guthrúnarson, Hrafn Guthrúnarson, Stein Herdísarson, Bersi Skáld-Torfuson, and Kormák Dolluson. (One is justified in including Kormák, though he is called Ogmundarson in the *Skáldatal* [Enumeration of Skalds], because in the Kormáks saga the two brothers at Mel, Kormák and Thorgils, are called "the sons of Dalla," even though their father is mentioned a few lines before.) At the same time, as might be expected, it is of great importance to find that the court skalds are closely related to personages who also are named after their mother. Thus the poets Sigvat Thórtharson, Thórth Sigvaldaskáld, and Óttar the Swart are all counted among the closest of kin to Hrafn, the son of Guthrún. The grandfather of Herdís, the mother of Stein, was the poet Einar skálaglamm, who again was the kinsman of the sons of Æsa and the sons of Thorhalla. Thórth Ingunnarson was the grandfather of the skald Stúf the Blind, and Thórth's father was the skald Glúm Geirason. The skald Vigfús Víga-Glúmsson is the son of a

---

[4] *Safn til Sögu Íslands* (Copenhagen, 1907–1915), IV, 585–910.

sister of Thorgrím Hlífarson and a kinsman of the skald Eyjólf Valgertharson. Skúli Thorsteinsson is the grandson of Gunnar Hlífarson.
Thorleif jarlaskáld (Earls' Skald), and the skalds Tind Hallkelsson,
Gunnlaug ormstunga (Serpent's Tongue), Hofgertha-Ref, Thórth
Kolbeinsson, and Arnór, his son, all claimed descent from kinsmen who
followed that strange custom of naming, though one cannot now point
out their close relatives who were named after their mother. Above I
have mentioned nineteen court skalds, but of twenty-five other court
poets we know some distinctive family traits besides the names of their
parents.

  We are probably not far wrong in stating that there are thirty-four
women who, in the history of Iceland before, and in the middle of, the
eleventh century share the honorable distinction that their sons bear
their mother's name as though they were patronymics. Three mothers
of landtake men are among them. Most of these women lived in the
districts of the West and Northland notable for producing skalds, but
in all of the Eastland, only two, possibly four. The four who may be
counted as being from the Eastland are Járngerth, Fjorleif, Mardoll, and
Droplaug. The second son of Droplaug of Arneitharstathir is one of the
few skalds of the Eastland known to us. According to the *Brandkrossa
thátt* (story), Mardoll must have been the grandmother of Droplaug;
but we can scarcely depend on this source. About Járngerth we know
only that she was the mother of Ófeig of Skarth, who is said to have
been the grandfather of Ófeig Skíthason. And Ófeig, the son of Járngerth, hailed from Gnúpafell in the Eyjafjall District and was a kinsman
of that notable family, so well endowed with poetic gifts, of Helgi the
Lean and Thórunn hyrna, daughter of the *hersir* Ketil Flatnose. Some
uncertainty exists whether Járngerth herself was of Eastland origin. On
the other hand, it is quite certain that Fjorleif hailed from Reykdale,
being the daughter of Eyvind, one of the first settlers, who was the son
of Thorstein hofthi, a *hersir* in Horthaland in Norway. Her husband,
Thórir Leatherneck, was by male descent a kinsman of Bjorn buna; and
from this *hersir* Bjorn buna, from Arinbjorn of the Fjord District of

Norway, from Úlf the Courageous, and from Ketil raum are descended some of the foremost families of Iceland endowed with poetic gifts. A granddaughter of Fjorleif was Guthrún, wife of Hrólf at Gnúpafell. And their son was the court skald Eilíf Guthrúnarson.

It is no exaggeration to say that in the times of the Old Icelandic skaldship every fifth man bearing a metronymic name could be reckoned a skald. That group occupies nearly every tenth seat of honor among them. This fact makes it altogether unnecessary to investigate any further the relationships of the thirty-four women mentioned above with the poets of old. So in heathen times a close relationship seems to have existed between the practice of skaldship and the custom of naming children after their mother. This important fact is seen to have many consequences.

Now, it ought to be understood that the Old Icelandic pursuit of skaldship is not to be regarded as the particular gift of individuals or even families, but rather as the distinctive characteristic of a definite class, a characteristic which was of great importance in our land yet never became dominant. Else how can it be explained that customs so diverse in nature as the composition of poetry, for one thing, and the designation of persons by their mother's name, for the other, go hand in hand in the same family and set their stamp on certain sections of the country so that their distinctive quality could be discerned down to the latest times?

It has long been understood that in times of yore poetry and magic went together; which fact furnishes an insight into one main aspect of Old Norse culture. What concerns Icelandic culture in heathen times, I have no doubt but that they are branches from the same root. It was the women connected with this strange custom of naming who convinced me of that. In the plain words of our sources, seven of them are said to have practiced witchcraft or black magic; and not one in that group had kinsfolk in or dwelled in the Eastland east of Vathla Heath. We hear of no wisewomen or seeresses engaged there in black magic in the olden times. We can hardly count among them Tófa hlítharsól (Sun of the

Slope) or the foster mother of Brodd-Helgi, even though they dreamed of the events of the coming day. In the sagas of the Eastland there is indeed mention of three women practicing black magic, but two of them dwelled by the shores of the Eyjafjord, in the landtake of Helgi the Lean, and the third, in foreign parts. We do find Old Icelandic sorceresses in the most flourishing sections of the country, and precisely those boasting of skalds. Indeed, there is no dearth of them there. Herein we may discover the distinctive feature of the particular culture in which skaldcraft thrived.

Among the skalds, then, and among the women practicing witchcraft the custom arose of naming children after their mother. Obviously, we may regard this custom as a sign of unusually pronounced women's rights among those families that followed it. It matters little that possibly this habit of naming prevailed especially where children had lost their father when young or were illegitimate. At the time our sources of information were written, this explanation of the custom is likely to have seemed the natural one. But it is important to find the causes or the origin of this custom, and no better explanation occurs to me than that it is likely to be one handed down in a branch of the human family which honored women more than was common among Germanic tribes. Certainly the residence of women practicing witchcraft precisely in neighborhoods where skalds abounded seems to point in a definite direction. But we must first explore various lines before going into that matter. First and foremost, it is necessary to ascertain, if possible, whether the independence of women in the olden times prevailed more in districts where skalds resided than in others. And though it may appear remarkable, yet we have fairly good evidence for answering this question positively.

"It was determined that a woman was not to take possession of more land than a two-year old heifer could walk around, when led on a spring day, between sunrise and sunset." Thus the Hauk Erlendsson version of the Book of Settlements expresses it.[5] This statement does not

---

[5] *Ldn.* § 362.

necessarily rest on fact, but shows all the same that historians assumed considerable participation of women in the settlement. The presumption arises that during the period of colonization women at times were the leading personages and in charge of a group. There are a great many examples of this. Thus Auth the Deep-minded, the daughter of Bjorn buna, progenitor of so many skalds, "was a very stately lady." She took possession of the entire Dalaland District, and she is counted one of the noblest and most powerful of those who took possession of land. Thorgerth, the widow of the *hersir* Ásbjorn Bjarnarson, and a kinswoman of Auth, took possession of the whole Oræfasveit District. Her granddaughter was temple priestess. So one may suppose that women were highly regarded in that family. For that matter, we likewise find a temple priestess in the Hvamm District, one of the hereditary landed possessions belonging to Auth's family. Yet only five women priests are known from the old sagas. Ásgerth, the daughter of *hersir* Ask, and grandmother of the skald Njál at Bergthórshvol, possessed herself of a huge tract of land in the Rangár District. She emigrated to Iceland with her brother, still she took possession of land in her own right. Ljót, who settled at Ljótharstathir, likewise emigrated with her brother and near relations; and also Thórunn, sister-in-law of *hersir* Ásgrim Úlfsson. Both these women were independent settlers.

In this connection we must mention Steinunn the Old, widow of Herlaug, of *hersar* rank, brother of Skalla-Grím. She did not want to accept land as a gift, "but gave for it a spotted English cloak with a hood, calling that a trade." Later on, she let her foster son and kinsman have a part of her landtake. Within Skalla-Grím's landtake four women settled, viz., Arnbjorg at Arnbjargarlœk (A. Brook), Thórunn in Thórunnarholt (Th. Woods), Thorbjorg in Stangarholt, and Thuríth the Seeress, her sister, at Grof (Ditch). Among the woman settlers may also be mentioned Geirríth in Borgardale, the grandmother of the wisewoman Geirríth in Mávahlíth (M. Slope), who was the mother of the skald Thórarin the Black. Two woman settlers are named as living by the Ísafjarthardjúp fjord, Thuríth sundafyllir (Sound-filler) and

Thúríth rúmgylta. The accounts of their landtake may be called most remarkable: The one took possession of land together with her son, the other, with her husband. Thuríth sundafyllir was a widely known and highly regarded wisewoman. It is told of her that once, when there was a famine in Hálogaland in Norway, she "filled every sound with herrings" by means of her witchcraft. "She located Kvíamith [a fishing bank] in the Ísafjarthardjúp fjord and took a polled ewe from every farmer along the Ísafjord [for that]." Her son was the skald Volu-Stein, who of course had that surname after her.[6] From Thuríth rúmgylta was descended the skald Ólaf bjarnylr (Bear's Warmth), who in one stanza is called the son of Bjargey. The last, but by no means the least, remarkable example of landtake women is Arndís the Wealthy, mother of Thórth of Múli. He was named Arndísarson after his mother. Arndís was the daughter of Steinólf the Short, the son of the *hersir* Hrólf, who took possession of land in the Saurbær District; but she chose for herself a piece of land along the Hrútafjord. She lived at Bær after Bálki, the ancestor of the skalds Holmgongu-Bersi and Bjorn Hitdœlakappi (Champion of the Hitdœlers). The accounts seem to point to there having been some connection between these skald families and Arndís and her son Thórth, but it is not known of what nature this kinship was.

We shall now turn our attention to Ljót, the woman landtaker dwelling at Ljótarstathir (L.-stead), Thorberg Stong (Rod), in Stangarholt (St.-woods), Arnbjorg, at Arnbjargarlœk (A. creek), and Thórunn, in Thórunnarholt. And now many parallels from the oldest accounts of the settlement of our land come to mind. Auth the Deep-minded dwelled first at Authartoptir (A.'s homestead). Langaholts-Thóra and Ásmund Atlason, her husband, lived at Thórutoptir until Ásmund divorced himself from Thóra "on account of the run of· visitors [to her], and went to live at Oxl." Of Thóra we are told that "she had a hall built athwart the common travelled road and always had a table standing there, while she sat outside and offered food to every one who cared to eat."[7] It was to be expected that farmsteads bore the name of

[6] *Vǫlva*: seeress, wisewoman.      [7] *Ldn.* § 122.

such women although they were married. Thórdís, the daughter of Súr and sister of the skald Gísli, descended from a line of *hersir* rank in Súrnadale (Norway), set up her household at Thórdísarstathir when she divorced herself from Bork the Stout. If one can believe what is told of her, she chose to have the management of her farm in her own hands rather than retire to live with her son Snorri at Helgafell, the chief quarters of the family. This reminds one of the high-minded widow of the skald Eyólf Valgertharson, who resided at the farm Hanakamb, even though her sons, Guthmund the Powerful and Einar of Thverá, were wealthy farmers in that district. The same may be said about Fjorleif, the mother of notable sons. In her old age she lived at Fjorleif-toftir (F.-homestead). As noted above, she was of *hersar* origin. Of *hersir* descent on her forefathers' side were also Signý Valbrandsdóttir (-daughter), a kinswoman of Sigurth Gunnhildarson, and Kjolvor, daughter-in-law of Snæbjorn, brother of Helgi the Lean. The farms Signýjarstathir and Kjolvararstathir are named after these women.

Ingunn, the daughter of Thórólf, lived at Ingunnarstathir in the Geiradale District. Her grandfather was Dala-Koll, who was said to be "a *hersir* in rank." On the sword side she was a close kin of the skald Holmgongu-Bersi, and she was married to the court skald Glúm Geirason. Their son was Thórth Ingunnarson. A next-door neighbor of hers, Thuríth drikkja, dwelled at Kinnarstathir. Her sons were named Kinnarsons after her. In the same neighborhood there lived also Gróa at Gróustathir, the *vǫlva* (seeress) Heimlaug at Volvustathir, and Bera, mother of the Berusons who dwelled by the shores of the Berufjord. At Torfustathir in the Mithfjord District there lived Torfa, mother of the court skald Bersi. Close by dwelled Thórey at Thóreyjargnúp (Th.-Peak) and her sister Gróa at Gróustathir in Vatnsdale. Both were reputed to be much skilled in magic. And far out on the Skagastrand, at Spákonufell, (Seeress' Mountain), we find the seeress Thórdís, re-nowned of old. Finally, though more could be adduced, we shall mention Arneith of Arneitharstathir, the wife of the landtaker Ketil Thithrandason. She was the great-grandmother of Grím Droplaugarson.

We have now cited a considerable number of women from the time of colonization who lived on farms bearing their names. Most of them were of families having skalds, were descended from *hersar,* or were skilled in magic. So the notion is not unfounded that among women of the olden times there was a very important group that enjoyed complete independence and was prominent in the cultural life of their time. We must not be misled by the circumstance that Christian historians often give unfavorable accounts of heathen sorceresses. They were, rather, ahead of others in relishing and practicing the hidden lore or metaphysics of those times. No doubt this kind of knowledge was then as highly valued as is philosophy and natural science in our time. The high regard placed on sorcery and magic is seen most clearly in the legends of the gods, in which Óthin himself and Freyja were considered supreme masters in these matters. But Óthin was not only the supreme leader of "the workers in magic." "He and his temple priests are called songsmiths, because this skill was originated with them in the northern lands," says Snorri Sturluson.[8] Here it is plain as a pikestaff that the chief skills of the same god, according to popular belief, were magic and the inditing of charms in verse: "Óthin spoke all in rimes, as that is called which now we call skaldship," as Snorri says still further.

So it is clear as daylight that for a thousand years the names of independent and enterprising women have lived in Icelandic farm names. In general, the names of farms having as their first element a woman's name show that at one time a woman lived there who attempted to provide for herself by her own strength. If the property is of large extent, we may suppose that the mistress of the farm was capable and had sufficient help. Among women of this caliber it no doubt occurred especially frequently that children were named after their mother rather than after their father. Now, we have seen above that this custom often was associated with persons practicing skaldship and those possessing hidden knowledge. Here, then, the threads are found

[8] *Ynglinga saga,* Chapter 6.

twisted together to form a strong cord, whose strength we shall now test thoroughly.

In the group of those Icelandic farm names which have a man's name or else a sobriquet as the first element, those constitute the overwhelming majority which have as their second element the suffix-*stathir* (-stead), at least if we except the groups of smallish farms. Now, most remarkably, it so happens that it has been found easy to determine, with a fair degree of accuracy, the age of this, the largest group of Icelandic farm names. Scholars are probably unanimous in allowing that the largest number of these farm names date from the oldest period of Icelandic history. Very rarely do they show the cultural influences which came in the wake of Christianity and the Church. Wherever that occurs we always see these names belonging to abandoned farms or to cotters' places on outlying farms. This is, of course, not a matter of accident: In general -*stathir* farms with extensive lands are older than the smallish farms of the same name group. Because of their size and fertility of soil they have by far more rarely than the smallish farms been abandoned or become cotters' property. For this reason we shall focus attention on them. Also, the names of smallish farms are by no means a measure of the independence or spirit of free enterprise of the women of old. At all times indigent widows and other lone women had to toil with husbandry, whether or no they liked to, and often without the active help or caretakership of men. Nevertheless, their names have been preserved in farm names.

The clear-sighted may now readily discern the implications of what is brought out above. If my investigation is on the right track, one may expect that a difference will show between different sections of the country as to the number of those -*stathir* farms named after women. In comparing, one is bound to count both the men -*stathir* and the women -*stathir* farms of our land, and then establish the proportion between the number of -*stathir* named after women and the total of such names in every section of the country. This will reveal that such farm names did not have the same distribution in all four Quarters, though many are found everywhere. For the purpose of comparison, I chose the handy Register of Farms (1847) edited by Jón Jónsson. I counted the men -*stathir* and the women -*stathir* which were inhabited at that time, then arranged them according to the ancestry of their owners, while following in my accounts Finnur Jónsson's list of -*stathir* farms in the *Collections for the History of Iceland*,[9] even though I cannot agree with him in all particulars. The farms in the Westland showing women's names accounted for 14.5 per cent (of all farms); those of Northland, for 12.2 per cent; those of Southland, for 10.1 per cent; whereas in Eastland there were only 7.9 per cent of such farms.

In my comparison I did not count in the -*stathir* farms on the Vestmanna Islands, because it is certain that the farms there named after women got their names only in the thirteenth century. On the other hand, it is right to point out that Finnur Jónsson counted as farms bearing women's names Dísastathir and Kolfreyastathir in the South Múla District, Dísastathir in the Árnes District, and Meithasthathir in the Gullbringu District, but omitted as not belonging to that group Torfustathir in Núpsdale and a farm with the same name in the Bolstatharhlíthur Parish. It is difficult to agree with that, though it does not make much difference. He thinks that Dísastathir has as its first element a woman's name, Dís, which is pure guesswork. The woman's name Dís must be termed practically unknown in these parts in earlier centuries. On the other hand, the belief in Dísir (as feminine divinities) was firmly rooted among the Icelanders in heathen times, and traces of that are found in place names, as Kålund has pointed out in his Description of Iceland.[10] Finnur Jónsson omitted from the group of -*stathir* farms the two Torfustathir with women's names because of his peculiar notion that they had originally been called Torfastathir. But this supposition is entirely unfounded: In the rent roll of Árni and Pál[11] these farms are

[9] *Safn til Sögu Íslands*, IV, 412–584.
[10] P. E. K. Kålund, *Bidrag til en historisk-topografisk Beskrivelse af Island* (Copenhagen, 1877), I, 538 f.
[11] *Jarthabók Árna Magnússonar og Páls Vídalíns* (Copenhagen, 1926), VIII, 57, 85, 363.

called Torfustathir, and we can hardly suppose that the—rare—woman's name Torfa was ever substituted for the man's name Torfi. For that matter, fact is stronger than fancy in that in recent times the exact opposite happened with both these farms. That is the case also with Torfustathir in the Mithfjord District, which was named after Skáld-Torfa, the mother of Bersi. I shall not here expatiate on Meithastath and Kolfreyjastath, but only refer to the statements by Hannes Thorsteinsson in the Yearbook of the (Icelandic) Archaeological Society for the year 1923.

Various observations might also be made on the list of -*stathir* farms with men's names as their first element, but I shall not do so in this brief treatment. A few additions to the number of farm names having men's names as their first element and those that do not, or have a sobriquet as first element, make little difference in the comparison which is to be made here. Taking into account the rectifications mentioned above, the proportional frequency in the four parts of the country of women's names with -*stathir* is as follows:

> Westland: 124; with women's names, 18 = 15.5%
> Northland: 222 .................. 29 = 13.1%
> Southland: 156 .................. 14 = 9%
> Eastland: 214 .................... 15 = 7%

It is manifestly not possible to make a sharp distinction between farm names in -*stathir* with women's names as first element which bear witness to the independence and high status of the women of old and those named after indigent and unmarried women. Still one may confidently say that most of the -*stathir* farms in the Eastland bearing women's names were decidedly poorish. If we leave out all -*stathir* farms which are assessed at less than ten hundred,[12] the Eastland will be seen to lag far behind the other Quarters. Then the number of such farms would total only 5 per cent there, whereas the percentage

[12] A hundred is the standard unit of real estate. Originally it meant 120 ells of homespun.

in other parts of the country would remain about the same. Put briefly: the Westland, so rich in skalds, has proportionally three times more *-stathir* farms named after women than the Eastland with its few skalds and small poetic production. This would be an extraordinary accident and most mysterious if there had not at one time been a close cultural correlation between skaldic skill and the rise of the larger *-stathir* farms called after women.

Magnus Olsen chose as a subject for discussion[13] the gross and exceedingly remarkable difference between the Norwegian and the Icelandic *-stathir* farm names. By his count there are known in Norway about 2,500, and in Iceland, about 1,100 farms which have as their first element a personal name or a sobriquet and *-stathir* as the second. He observes that more than one in every ten Icelandic *-stathir* names has as its first element a woman's name, as against only thirty such in Norway, including doubtful ones; in fact, that it probably would be nearer the truth to cut that number in half. It is not surprising that this most eminent scholar, so rich in ideas, would not silently pass by this startling difference between the two countries in the number of woman *-stathir* names, but try to account for it. He is of the opinion that the different ages of the *-stathir* farms of Iceland and those of Norway is the chief reason, as well as the unlike conditions for husbandry in the two countries. He seems to consider that a great number of farms bore the name of indigent women who to some extent, or not at all, depended on the help of men in their farm work. These attempts to explain the fact have troubled me, because they very likely make it clear how it is that a very exact and intelligent man did not train his eyes on the heart of the matter. The deeply rooted old belief that the Icelandic people and their ancient culture are chiefly derived from Norway has obscured the view. Like the storied helm of invisibility (or causing invisibility), it has for centuries settled over various important problems of Old Norse history, turning daylight into darkness and sunshine into shadow. As soon as this spirit of darkness is dispelled we do not need to ask why

13 *Farms and Fanes of Ancient Norway* (Oslo, 1928), pp. 97 f.

Icelandic -*stathir* farms named after women are proportionally almost seventeen times more numerous than the Norwegian ones. We quietly reverse the attack and say: this important difference shows that Icelandic women of old enjoyed by far more liberty of action and respect than their kindred sisters in Norway.

After the Settlement of Iceland came to an end Norway was for centuries almost without skalds. Poetry which had been composed before was forgotten, barring what was preserved by the emigrants that peopled Iceland. And it seems most probable that it was precisely those families characterized by producing skalds who preserved the fruits of that poetic culture, viz., the Eddic lays of gods and heroes as well as other poems, besides others which did not endure. In the Viking Period it was a veritable fashion, in both Norway and Iceland, to give farms names ending in -*stathir* and to distinguish them by the names of the occupants. Among such farms, those in Norway with women's names are found to number only 1 per cent, or more likely, something like 0.6 per cent; whereas in Iceland they number about eleven out of every hundred. Too, in Iceland the Eastland had both the fewest skalds and the fewest -*stathir* farms with women's names. Also, scarcely any lays were treasured there in people's minds.

## 2. Skalds, Swine, Saur- Farms

Heithnarey Island is a small, uninhabited island in the Breithafjord, off Skálmarness. In those parts there lived in men's minds a peculiar tradition connected with this island. After the Conversion, secret heathen sacrifices were permitted, for the first. The farmer living at Múli on Skálmarness undertook, for a proper consideration, to ferry people who wished to sacrifice in secret over to the island. The sacrifices were performed at the beginning of the fifth month of summer. To support this story, people used to point out a little valley and a hollow in it which bore the names of Blóthvammur (Grassy Slope Where Sacrifices Were Performed) and Saurlífisgjá (Cleft of Unclean Living). Thus Kålund[1] has it from a tradition which probably was put down in writing in fairly early times. Unfortunately, I did not have the opportunity to find out more about the sources for this information.

Most likely, it seems, the secret sacrifices on Heithnarey Island were connected with harvest festivals, or festivities after the hay had been garnered, and were brought to propitiate the fertility gods, Frey and Freyja. Whatever one may think about the validity of the tradition, the place name Saurlífisgjá reminded me of an old and forgotten observation Guthbrand Vigfússon once made about the *saur*- place names and the worship of Frey and Freyja. In his treatise "On the Chronology of the Sagas of Icelanders"[2] he has this to say when recalling the emigration to Iceland of Thorbjorn súr of Súrnadale (Norway). "We hold it

---

[1] P. E. K. Kålund, *Bidrag til en historisk-topografisk Beskrivelse af Island* (Copenhagen, 1877), I, 538 f.

[2] "Um Tímatal í Íslendinga Sögum," in *Safn til Sögu Íslands* (Copenhagen, 1856), I, 363.

to be true that wherever in Iceland or Norway place names like these are found, there sacrifices were made to Frey, that belief in Frey and Freyja was greater there than at other places, and also that whole districts took their name from this, as e.g. Saurar (S. farm), Sýrstrands, Súrnadale, -Sýr (Sow) being one of the goddess Freyja's names. And this proves to be true also in the case of the Sýrdalers, in that they made great sacrifices [to Frey]. When we hear that the *gothi* Thorgrím was so acceptable to Frey, the likelihood is that he continued the sacrifices his kinsmen had made; because it is nowhere stated that the Thorsness people sacrificed to Frey but on the contrary were great devotees of Thór. We also think that Thorbjorn súr had his name from being a worshipper of Frey, and that people in his native district in Norway were great believers in Frey."

Undeniably, this train of reasoning does not go very far. Yet Guthbrand Vigfússon's opinion about the connection between the Súr-, Saur-, Sýr- place names and Frey and Freyja worship has not been heeded by scholars. In spite of that, it may well be that the presentiment of that keen student here, as so many times elsewhere, hit the mark. At least, I consider it a matter of course to give closer attention than has so far been done to the above cited observation. One's mind then presently adverts to the narrative of the Eyrbyggja saga[3] about the fight between the Kjalleklings and Thorstein, the father of Thorgrím the *gothi*, about the sanctity of the place of assembly on Thorsness. This account is so characteristic and exceptional that it is worth while here to quote the text verbally. To explain the circumstances, though, it should be stated first that both the Kjalleklings and the Thorsness people shared the place where the assembly was held; but it was Thórólf Mostrarskegg who, when settling at Thorsness, had assigned the place for the district assembly. "That was so sanctified a spot that he would not permit it to be defiled in any manner whatever, and men were not to ease themselves there. For that purpose a skerry was set aside which was called Excrement Skerry." After Thórólf's death

[3] Chapters 9 and 10.

Thorstein thorskabít, his son, kept up the same observance about the sanctity of the place of assembly.

"It happened one spring at the Thorsness Assembly that Thorgrím Kjallaksson and his brother-in-law, Ásgeir of Eyr, declared they would no longer put up with the arrogance of the Thorsness people. They said furthermore that they would ease themselves there on the grass as anywhere else at meetings, even though those people were so haughty that they considered their lands more sacred than other farms in the Breithafjord region. They made it known that they would not wear out their footgear wading out to an outlying skerry for easing themselves. But when Thorstein thorskabít heard of this he declared he would not tolerate their defiling with their excrements the field which his father Thórólf had revered above all other spots on his lands. He summoned his friends, intending to keep the others from the field by force if they meant to defile it."—"Now in the evening, when the Kjalleklings had finished their meal, they armed themselves and walked in the direction of the promontory. But when Thorstein saw that they turned off from the path leading to the skerry they seized their weapons and ran after them with challenging shouts."—"A fierce skirmish ensued between them."—"Some were killed on either side, but more of the Kjalleklings, and many were wounded."—"After the assembly both parties kept a large body of men under arms, and there was much suppressed enmity between them. Mutual friends then decided to send for Thórth gellir, who at that time was the greatest chieftain around the Breithafjord. He was a kinsman of the Kjalleklings, but also a close relative by marriage of Thorstein."—"The conclusion of the matter was that Thórth should arbitrate, but with these conditions: the Kjalleklings stipulated that they would never go to the Dirtskerry for their needs, while Thorstein declared that they must not defile the field now any more than before."—"Thórth made this the first point in his decision that each party should keep the advantage they had gained, neither party claiming compensation for the deaths and wounds which had been inflicted on Thorsness. Furthermore he declared that the field had been defiled by the bloodshed which had occurred there, so that the ground there was no more sacred there than anywhere else, and that they were the cause of it who had started the fight. That by itself, he said, had been a breach of the peace. He decided also that assemblies were to be held there no more."—"The place for the assembly was then moved farther inland on the promontory to its present site. And when Thórth gellir created the quarter assemblies he decided that the assembly of the Westfjords should be held there."—"This assembly site was held in extreme veneration, but people were not forbidden to ease themselves there."

The above account bears unusually distinct earmarks of relating events truthfully. Though it may be doubtful whether the author of the saga had a clear idea of the heart of the matter, yet one may unquestionably depend on the main points of his narrative. Father and son, Thórólf Mostrarskegg and Thorstein thorskabít are declared to be fervent worshippers of Thór and believed that the Thorsnessings would at death enter Helgafell Mountain. They had so great a reverence for the mountain "that no one was to look at it unwashed. No one was to be slain on it, neither cattle nor human beings, except what died there of its own accord." Thus this family has its distinct characteristics in tradition. Likewise, it is evident that the neighboring chieftains in Bjarnarhaven and at Hvamm had other religious tenets and customs than those of the Thorsnessings. Just like the worshippers of Frey in the Oræfa District, both the Kjalleklings and the people of Hvamm were descended from the line of Bjǫrn buna. For this reason the idea suggests itself that the cultural conditions and views of life of these closely related families were in the main the same. Also, it is among the Freygythlings[4] and the people of Hvamm that we find temple priestesses. But as Magnus Olsen has demonstrated,[5] it was precisely women priests who functioned in the religious activities of the Frey worshippers. Taking all this into account, the efforts to preserve

---

[4] For this family name and others, see *Ldn.*, index.
[5] *Farms and Fanes of Ancient Norway* (Oslo, 1928), p. 291.

the sanctity of the assembly grounds on Thorsness are not difficult to explain.

It is of course altogether improbable that the Kjalleklings out of sheer mischievousness caused the commotion on Thorsness. The arbiter, Thórth gellir puts the chief blame for what had happened on the Thorsnessings. Yet he was "a close relative by marriage" of Thorstein thorskabít. The author of the saga emphasizes that on the new and sacrosanct assembly grounds for the Quarter on Thorsness "it was permitted for any one to ease himself." That bloody fray resulting from the desecration of the sacrosanct meeting ground is calculated to have occurred in the years about 930. In 964 the assembly for the Quarter was established. What is the reason for people now being permitted to ease themselves on the hallowed assembly grounds? The most likely supposition is that there was a change in the religious beliefs and habits of the Thorsnessings. This supposition is confirmed by the author of the Gísla saga in his account of the Frey worship of the *gothi* Thorgrím, the son of Thorstein thorskabít.[6] Thorstein died by drowning when still young. His sons were brought up under the care of their mother, who was the sister of Thórth gellir. And, as might be expected, the young Thorsnessings, taking to the ways of their mother's kinsmen, inclined to the worship of the fertility gods; and forthwith the conflict between the faiths of their families comes to an end. It is safe to cite the violent hatred and the bloodshed because of *álfrek* (excrements, which drive the elves away) as a clear example of a conflict between different religious beliefs. That is the heart of the matter in the strange account of the Eyrbyggja saga about the battle on Thorsness.

The word *álfrek* seems to derive from some kind of belief in the hidden powers of *saur*. A reflection of such a belief may be seen also in the popular tradition of Witch-Manga,[7] as well as in the saying: "If one

[6] Chapter 18.
[7] Galdra-Manga. See Jón Árnason, *Íslenzkar pjóthsögur og Æventýri* (Leipzig, 1862), I, 517.

is inclined to be dirty (*saursæll*), he will be wealthy (auðsæll)." But, as we know, Frey was the god of wealth and was called *fégjafi* (Wealth Giver). Guthbrand Vigfússon seems to base his conclusion about the connection of the *saur-* place names and the belief in Frey and Freyja chiefly on the relationship between the words *saur*, *súr*, and *Sýr*, one of the goddess Freyja's names. I do not trust myself to judge about the etymology of these words, but one can readily note what the dictionaries say about the meaning of the word *saur* in the various Scandinavian languages. And this may well add up to an explanation, because the meanings of this word are remarkably multifarious. Thus: "marshland, mire, quagmire, excrements, urine, mud, semen, seed (to be sown), weeds in the fields, weed seed." Again, *saur* and *saura* are the names of some marsh and wet-land plants. In our country, however, the main significations of the word seem to have been "wet land, excrements, semen, mud." Doubtless all these meanings are from heathen times. At first sight, it might seem strange that conceptions so unrelated should be designated by the same word. But when we examine them more closely, the reason will be clear. The discovery that the hay recovery is better where manure is borne out on the field is older than the author of the Njáls saga makes it out to be. In the far distant past human beings endowed with some intelligence were bound to observe that excrements and watering promoted the growth of plants. For this reason a close connection is likely to have arisen in men's minds between excrements; fertile, well-watered land; swamp herbs; and light-green quagmires. They all receive the same designation, one reflecting fertility. *Saur* as the same word for seeds and human semen plainly is of identical origin. Where the vital force and the growing season were most clearly evident, there our primitive forebears imagined the divinity of fecundity to reside. And this being was at one time called *Saur* and worshipped. In ancient Scandinavian tradition we find it incorporated in the shape of the dog *Saur* figuring as king. Erp the Stooped, the progenitor of the Gilsbekkings, redeemed his head with a lay about this dog Saur when he had the misfortune of slaying a man in a sanctuary. That temple was hallowed to the dog Saur, and therefore his head-ransom dealt with that dog.

*Saur* as the designation of dirt now deserves our attention in larger measure. This specific sense of the word is hardly very old, especially as used of both spiritual and bodily uncleanliness. That innovation very likely is to be regarded as the telltale of churchly cultural influence on an ancient religious conception. Seen from this point of view, it is very easily understood why *saur* underwent such an unpleasant development as turned out to be the case. The heathen belief in *saur* undoubtedly was closely related to the life of the clan, and therefore was bound to provoke the bitterest antipathy of Christians. "To do sacrifice to [or worship] the holy gods" is the expression used in a stanza of the Ragnar saga[8] of the intercourse between man and woman. This expression points to an ancient connection between offering sacrifice and *saurlíf* (fornication). Students have reasons for believing that in Sweden, on the occasion of sacrifices to Frey, sexual intercourse took place as a kind of ritual. Parallel examples are well known in the religions of the Orient. It need not, therefore, be considered strange that the Cleft of Unclean Living and the Grassy Slope of Sacrifice lie side by side on Heithnarey Island and reminded people for a long time of the secret sacrifices made there every year at the beginning of the fifth month of summer.

If the word *saur* had sounded as offensive to the ears of heathens as to their Christian posterity, no one is likely to have designated his homestead in such unsavory fashion. I suspect indeed that occasionally people tried to rid their farms of their *saur-* names. There is a cotter's place at Sakka in Svarfathardale which originally was called Saurbæ-jarkot (Saurfarm Cot). From this it may be inferred what was the former name of the manor. For that matter, the known names of farms bearing the word *saur-* as their first element are tolerably numerous in our country. In the farm registry of 1847 twenty-eight are so called. Thus: sixteen Saurbær (S. farms), eight Saurar, one Saurbæjarkot (S. cot), one

[8] *Ragnars sage Lothbrókar*, Chapter 5.

Saurbrúargerthi (S. causeway, fence), one Saurlátur (S. lair), and one
Saurhóll (S. hill). Additionally, it is certain that there existed a Saurbær
in the Dalasýsla Parish, one in Svarfathardale, and one in the West
Skaptafell District. According to ancient tradition, the last-mentioned
Saurbær was the site of a church; and about four other *saur-* farms, we
know with certainty that they had been sites of churches during many
centuries.

Now, it is the opinion of notable scholars that churches were apt to
be built on the sites of heathen sanctuaries, or else close by them.[9] This
view is strongly supported by the history of the island of Gothland in
ancient times. The Icelandic *-hof* (temple) farms also are excellent
examples of this. Ólaf Lárusson has studied the number of former
churchstead farms among the various groups of farm names in our
country. Of *-hof* farms, 37.5 per cent proved to be sites of churches.
Next numerous were farm names in *-fell* (mountain), *ca.* 13.2 per cent.
After these came the groups of farms with *-eyri* (gravel bank), *-holt*
(wood), *-dal* (dale), *-bær* (farmhouse) as their last element. Of the last
named, 8.6 per cent had *church-* as their first element. Let us now examine the *saur-* farms. Of these, those with *-church* make up 26.4 per cent,
which is proportionally by half more than farm names containing both
the elements *-church* and *-fell*. We must, however, take into consideration that the old belief in the divinity of mountains may have had
something to do with the choice of some *-church* stead names. At the
same time, we have to reckon with the fact that most of the *saur-* farms
of which we are not sure whether they were *-church* farms are located
very close to former churches. Concerning one of them we know for
certain that there was a chapel formerly.

About the origin of the Saurbær farm in the Dalasýsla Parish we
possess a clear account in the Book of Settlements:[10] "Steinólf the
Short, the son of the *hersir* Hrólf in Agthir (Norway), took land from
the Klofa Stones to Grjótvallarmúli, and dwelled in Fagra Dale at

[9] See *Nordisk Kultur*, Vol. V (Stockholm, 1939), pp. 67 f.
[10] *Ldn.* § 165.

Steinólfshjalli. He entered into the mountains, and inside of them he saw a large valley all overgrown with woods. He detected a clearing in that valley. There he had his farmhouse built and called it Saurbær, because there was much boggy ground, and he gave the same name to the entire valley.—Steinólf also took possession of Steinólfs Dale in the Króksfjord District." Thereupon he moved to Bær.

Saurbær is not described as a swampy district. Still Steinólf chooses a site for his farm in the clearing which had "much boggy ground." He himself appears not to have stayed at Saurbær; and there in the swamp no farm maintained itself until fairly recently. This strange account may throw light on the origin of the Icelandic *saur-* farms. We may regard it as certain that the worshippers of the fertility gods held these divinities in reverence and prayed to both them and the holy wights of groves and *keldur* (quagmires). From the descriptions of farms one may clearly see that on the lands of the *saur-* farms there is an abundance of water, of mud, and of bog holes, which often caused the loss of live stock. It is especially in such places that people of old thought gods and other beings they believed in to reside, and therefore made votive offerings there or deposited in the ground valuables and animals they sacrificed. It is instructive in this connection to consider an account given in the Flóamanna saga.[11] At that time Christianity came to Iceland, and Thorgils was among the first to accept it. One night he dreamed that Thór appeared to him, looking angry, and reproached him for having failed him—"You have behaved badly to me," he said, "choosing for me the most worthless things you owned, and throwing the silver that belonged to me into a foul pond, and I shall turn against you."—And when Thorgils awoke he saw that his home-fed boar was dead. He had it buried near some homestead and did not permit it to be eaten. Again Thór appeared to Thorgils in a dream and said that "it would be no harder for him to suffocate Thorgils than his boar . . . ."

The kernel of truth in this confused account is obvious. At sites where in ancient times sacrifices were made there persist memories of

[11] *Flóamanna saga*, Chapter 20.

such offerings. There, silver was dropped into swamps, and home-fed boars, consecrated to the gods, were buried in the ground. Sacrificial customs such as these are well known from the history of other lands. The great finds of silver from the olden times, especially in the Baltic provinces of Scandinavia, amply support the existence of this custom. Gudmund Schütte[12] mentions the fact that until recently the farmers of Kongsted on the island of Seeland in Denmark were accustomed to bury live cows and then to dance and have all sorts of merriment above the place of burial. They let the animal to be sacrificed suffer the agony of death by suffocation: so unalterably fixed were the Kongsted farmers in their age-old ritual of sacrifice. This instance reminds one strongly of the death and burial of the home-fed boar in the Flóamanna saga. We may now discern the strands of which the account of it were woven, even though it may be distorted considerably.

The home-fed boar and the harvest festivities assuredly are intimately connected. If I am not mistaken, the Icelandic harvest rites derive from similar ones in heathen times. Keeping this in mind, the designation *saur* for the manure carted on the fields becomes even clearer in its religious implications. It is from this manure that the home field obtains its great power of growth. The home-fed boar is fattened so well that "it can scarcely get on its feet." Through him is to be repaid the strength of the growing season and the prolific growth of the home-field hay. At the harvest festivals of the ancient Greeks, Demeter, the goddess of agriculture, was worshipped with sacrifices of swine which were buried in the ground. Sacrificial burials are known also in our country. They are mentioned by the author of the Vatnsdæla saga in his account of Thórólf heljarskin in the Forsælu Valley.[13] From the popular beliefs and old cults in South Sweden we may infer that in the olden times there existed a very close connection between the harvest feast, swine worship, and the adoration of Frey. It is certain that the ancient worship of swine was interwoven with the worship and

[12] Gudmund Schütte, *Hjemligt Hedendom* (Copenhagen, 1919), p. 127.
[13] *Vatnsdæla saga*, Chapter 16.

adoration of the powers of fecundity. The boar was the animal sacred to Frey and Freyja, with Freyja herself being called Sýr (sow). This matter has been thoroughly investigated by Helge Rosén in the Swedish journal *Fornvennan*, 1913.

The accounts of the sacrificial burials of Thórólf heljarskin and that of the home-fed boar which was buried "near some homestead" may perhaps seem of little moment. To me they became guideposts, pointing my thoughts to the problem whether the swine sacrifices in our country did not take place chiefly in the districts having *saur-* farms, and whether the worshippers of the fertility gods dwelled especially in those tracts. Thórólf heljarskin lived a short distance from Saurbær in Vatnsdale; and close by, in the Villingahólt Parish, probably lived some of Thorgils orrabeinstjúp's descendants, his who owned the home-fed boar killed by Thór. Among them were skalds and history writers like Skeggi Bjarnarson in Grǫf and his sons. It is likely that in this family most of the accounts about Thorgils were preserved. The *Flóamanna saga* bears some witness to this.

In addition to the account about the home-fed boar, I have encountered in the sources dealing with the Settlement and the saga times fourteen stories about swine, five of them in the Book of Settlements. Of the boar which Hrafnkel Freysgothi owned we are told that it perished in an avalanche.[14] Of the swine of Geirmund heljarskin it is said that "they fed on Swínaness."[15] Oddi ýrarson, his daughter's son, was married to a *gyðja* (priestess), and on the home grounds of Geirmund at Skarth there grew a rowan tree grove in some swamp, and some belief was connected with it. Both of these traditions point to a fertility cult in Geirmund's family. Steinólf the Short, the one who built Saurbærfarm in the Saurbær neighborhood, "lost three swine. They were found two years later in Svínadale, and numbered 30 then."[16] Helgi the Lean "put two swine ashore, a boar called Sölvi and a sow.

---

[14] *Hrafnkels saga Freysgotha*, Chapter 1.
[15] *Ldn.* § 164.
[16] *Ldn.* § 165.

They turned up three years later in Sölvadale, and then numbered 70."[17] Sölvadale is in the Saurbær Parish along the Eyjafjord. The first mistress in the Saurbær farm there was Helga, the daughter of Helgi the Lean. One may infer from the account given in the Ljósvetninga saga that the former inhabitants of the old Saurbær farm owned a mountain pasture in Sölvadale. One of the Saurbær farms was built on the land-take of Ingimund the Old, quite near the home pastures of the people at Hof: "ten swine disappeared from Ingimund's farm. They were found in the following fall, and they then numbered one hundred. The boar was called Beigath. He jumped into Svínavatn Lake and swam till his cloven feet came off. He died [from overexertion] on Beigatharhvól (B. knoll)."[18] The above are the accounts about swine that occur in the Book of Settlements.

As is well known, the action of the Harthar saga takes place in the environs of Saurbær by the Hvalfjord. Two stories are told in it about swine. The people of Hólm collected "the swine of the farmers in Svínadale, drove them down to the strand, killed them there, and carried the carcasses onto their ship. That place is now called Svína-sandur [S. sand or shore]." It was the farmers of the Saurbær Parish from whom they were stolen. The Hólm people had quarreled with the sorceress Skroppa in Saurbær. They made for her, but Skroppa employed optical illusions (with her magic) and changed herself and the two daughters of the farmer at Saurbær into the likeness of swine.[19] Similar stories are handed down in the Eyrbyggja saga and the Thorsk-firthinga saga. In the former saga we read that Katla at Hólt brought it about by her optical illusions that to Arnkel *gothi* it seemed that a home-fed boar lay under the refuse heap at Hólt, whereas it really was Odd, Katla's son.[20] In the Thorskfirthinga saga[21] we are told that Askmathr and Katla transformed themselves into swine. A similar account we

[17] *Ldn.* § 265.
[18] *Ldn.* § 226.
[19] *Harthar saga*, Chapters 26 and 29.
[20] *Eyrbyggja saga*, Chapter 20.
[21] *Thorskfirthinga saga* (or *Gull-Thóris saga*), Chapter 10.

find there about Thuríthr drikkin. All three, Askmathr, Katla, and Thuríthr lived near Steinólf the Short, in both the saga and their actual dwelling places. In the Vatnsdæla saga we are told that when Thorkel krafla lived in Forsæludale with Klakka-Orm, at one time he gathered together the swine and a shoat ready for slaughter to take them down from the mountains. This account is linked with the wedding feast which was to take place "at Forsæludale at the time of the winter nights [i.e., at the beginning of the winter season]."[22] In the Valla-Ljóts saga[23] we are told that Hrethu-Halli's mother had sent him to farmer Torfi at Torfufell after a pig. She was at that time engaged to Torfi, and "the wedding was to take place in the winter nights." Torfufell farm is in the Saurbær Parish. A swine is mentioned also in the Víga-Glúms saga[24] at Jorunnarstathir in the same district. That was a home-fed boar "so fat that he could hardly get up." Its owner was Halli the White, the son of Thorbjorn, who was the son of the daughter of Helga at Saurbær. Finally a boar is mentioned in the Svarfdæla saga.

These stories about swine are worthy of our attention. The one swine mentioned in the sagas of the Eastland was owned by the "Freys*gothi*" Hrafnkel. The tales about the swine herds of Steinólf the Short, Ingimund the Old, and Helgi the Lean are, with regard to substance, cast in the same mold, and therefore the same explanation fits them all. The author of Vatnsdæla saga has provided us with one. He reports somewhat more fully than do the authors of the Book of Settlements of the disappearance of Ingimund's swine. "It is said that some of Ingimund's swine disappeared and were not found until the second summer toward fall, when they numbered a hundred. A big old boar called Beigath was with them. Ingimund summoned people to catch them, and said it was correct to say that there were two heads on each. They went after the swine and drove them to the lake which now is called Svínavatn (Swine lake) and intended to pen them there, but the

---

[22] *Vatnsdæla saga*, Chapter 42.
[23] *Valla-Ljóts saga*, Chapter 1.
[24] *Víga-Glúms saga*, Chapter 17.

boar jumped into the lake and swam across it, but became so tired that his cloven feet came off him. He got to the shore at Beigatharhvól [B. hill] and expired there. *Now Ingimund felt happy in Vatnsdale.*" The powers of fertility had plainly shown to him that their blessing lay on these parts. The fecundity, endurance, and the recovery of the swine which had disappeared was a visible token of that. Helgi and Ingimund gave their boars men's names. The boars Beigath and Sölvi were the chosen animals of Frey and Freyja, and they had proved equal to their task.

Accounts like these are bound to originate among fertility worshippers, and we do not need to turn many pages to be convinced that both the Vatnsdæla people and the Eyfirthings rendered homage to the fertility cult. The author of the Víga-Glúms saga[25] speaks plainly about the Frey sanctuary of the kinsmen of Helgi the Lean as having been located at Hripkelsstathir, and is explicit in his accounts, which bear the clearest witness to their worship of Frey. The author of the Vatnsdæla saga refers to Ingimund the Old's having carried an image of Frey in his pouch, and calls his daughter-in-law a priestess. These statements are not at all surprising: Both Helgi and Ingimund trace back their ancestry to Sweden, the principal land of the Frey worship. Now it becomes evident why the traditions and other cultural reminiscences in the Vatnsdale and the Eyjafjarthar District are so remarkably similar.

I shall cite some examples. During his first winter in Iceland Ingimund resided in Vithidale in the Northland. "But when it became spring and the snow thawed on the mountain slopes, Ingimund said: 'I wonder if some men would climb a high mountain and find out if there was less snow in other places.' They did so and saw 'mountains without snow in the southeast,' and told Ingimund. 'But it looks as though the same snowstorm prevailed here all the time, and we can see that the quality of the land there is much better.' Ingimund answered: 'Then it is all right; but let us wait still and see if something favorable may lie ahead of us. Useless to struggle against fate!' Early in spring Ingimund removed himself from Vithidale to Vatnsdale."[26]

[25] *Ibid.*, Chapter 5.          [26] *Vatnsdæla saga*, Chapter 15.

During his first winter in Iceland Helgi the Lean dwelled on the outer Árskógsstrands. "They had a severe winter so that the livestock they had with them was on the point of death. But in the spring Helgi went up on Sólarfjall Mountain and saw that inside the fjord the ground looked more snowfree by far. He carried all his possessions onto his ship and journeyed to those parts. During Helgi's removal of his household to Kristness his wife, Thórunn hyrna, gave birth to a girl child on Thórunnarey Island in one of the branches of the Eyjafjord, and the child was called Thorbjorg hólmasól [Sun of the Islet]."[27] The same happened to Vigdís, the wife of Ingimund. When the couple and their company "arrived in Vatnsdale Vigdís declared: 'Here I shall tarry, because I feel the pangs of childbirth.' Ingimund made answer: '*May that be a good omen.*' Then Vigdís gave birth to a girl child. It was called Thórdís. Ingimund declared: 'This place shall be called Thórdísarhólt (Th. Wood).' Thereupon the company proceeded up the valley and saw that the quality of the soil was good and that there was herbage and forest. Then the company became very cheerful."[28] The birth of the girl child by the Vatnsdale River had given them a fair promise, which was fulfilled before they expected it.

It was in Vithidale that to Ingimund's men it seemed "as though the same snowstorm prevailed all the time." And along the Árskógsstrands Helgi's livestock was about to perish, owing to the severity of the last three months of winter. It was in these localities that the landtakers had built their homes to begin with. They had the same experience as Gnúpa-Bárthi, the brother of Ásbjorn and the progenitor of the Freysgythlings. He did not seek shelter from the northern on-land winds of late winter before he had lived for a while at Lundarbrekka. "Then he observed that the land winds were milder than the sea winds and he considered that there was the chance of better land south of the mountains."[29] He thereupon removed to the Fljótshverfi District. This

27 *Ldn.* § 265.
28 *Vatnsdæla saga*, Chapter 15.
29 *Ldn.* § 289.

observation of the climate shows that the families of Bárthi, Helgi, and Ingimund had dwelled for some time in the land (i.e., Norway) where the sea breeze brought thaws and mild rains which cut short severe winters and prepared the way for the growth of the spring vegetation. The fertility gods governed sunshine, rain, and winds. Their worshippers, when first they arrived, chose their domiciles by the open sea. They came to grief on their choice of habitation in the Northland of Iceland. There, the persistent sea winds did not bring them mild weather with sufficient and early spring growth, but on the contrary, cold weather and hardship. The recollection of the sore disappointment of the fertility worshippers who thought themselves forsaken by good fortune is mirrored in the removal of Ingimund and Helgi from their unpropitious location. The powers had ceased sending the landtakers the mild spring winds; the gods themselves had forsaken their worshippers. But before they expected it, guidance was lent them to better fortunes and prosperity. Land with less snow was beheld by them to the south. That was the promised land. And as soon as they had arrived there, the wives of the landtakers gave birth to girl children, and the half-starved swine fattened quickly and multiplied their kind in a very short time.

It is hardly necessary to state why the above-mentioned accounts are associated with the names of the men who hailed from the same region (in the old country). This is a plain example of how one may infer the cultural conditions and the religious life of heathen people from the distinctive traditions which their offspring preserved. And these features, shared by both the Vatnsdæla people and the Eyfirthings, on the whole bear witness to the fertility cults of both families. They were sun worshippers. Thorkel krafla, the *gothi* of the Vatnsdælers, is quoted as saying of the sons of Ingimund: "They believed in him who created the sun and governs all things." The names Sólarfjall (Sun Mountain) and Hólmasól allow us to infer the same about the sun worship of the Eyfirthings. And it is instructive to note how firmly such traditions are associated with the fertile tract Eyjarengi (Island Meadow) in Vatnsdale and the field Vitathsgjafi (Sure Giver) in the Eyjafjǫrd District. Both of these were located in the home district of the descendants of Ingimund and of Helgi.

With the same distinctive characteristics of these families in mind, it will prove easier to obtain a clearer insight into the accounts about swine and the cultic value of these accounts. It will not do to ignore the fact that the legends about the hog of Torfi at Torfufell and the gathering of the swine of Thorkel krafla in Forsæludale are reminiscences of the worship of the fertility gods in Vatnsdale and the Eyjafjord District. Both accounts are told in the same fashion as was the above-mentioned wedding assignment for the "winter nights." The authors of the Valla-Ljóts saga and Vatnsdæla saga appear not to have had any notion of the relation which originally existed between the stories about swine and the weddings to be celebrated. According to Adam of Bremen, the sacrifices to Frey among the Swedes took place at the same time as marriages.[30] Doubtless on such occasions swine were sacrificed. They were the most prolific of domestic animals and therefore a most fitting sacrifice, on such occasions dedicated to Frey and Freyja. Again, we may satisfactorily explain why weddings were set on the "winter nights": That was the time to perform the sacrifice to Frey. "Thorgrím intended to have the autumn celebration during the 'winter nights' and make a feast to welcome winter and to make sacrifice to Frey."[31] Thus the author of Gísla saga about the *gothi* Thorgrím Thorsteinsson. Now it is clear why Thorkel krafla goes collecting the swine and why Hrethu-Halli is sent to fetch the pig right before the wedding in the "winter nights."

Now we shall take a closer look at the four accounts about swine in connection with sorceresses or which deal with shape shifting or optical illusions. As between wizardry and such phenomena the difference could hardly have been great. Snorri Sturluson has this to say about

---

[30] Adamus Bremensis (*ca.* 1045–1076), *Historia Hammaburgensis Ecclesiæ*, Book IV, Chapter 27.
[31] *Gísla Saga Súrssonar*, Chapter 15.

Freyja: "She was a heathen priestess, who first among the Æsir instruc-
ted in magic, which was customary with the Vanir."[32] This tradition is
likely to have originated where sacrifices to Freyja, witchcraft, and
powerful magic were associated. Sorceresses as a rule were dedicated
Freyja worshippers, and so naturally made an idol of swine above other
animals, seeing that Freyja was the swine goddess and swine were
animals sacred to Freyja. Accounts about swine and witches thus point
to a fervent worship of fertility in the parts where they originated. It is
the Vatnsdæla saga, the Thorskfirthinga saga, the Harthar saga, and the
Eyrbyggja saga which have preserved most of the accounts about
swine and sorceresses. There we find seven accounts about swine, and
sixteen witches are mentioned. These four sagas of Icelanders all agree
in dealing especially with chieftains of *saur-* farm districts and their
neighbors. In these tracts reminiscences of swine in the olden times and
the sorcery of women are along the same lines. There can be no mistake
about that.

Nine of the fifteen accounts about swine which we have discussed are
localized in *saur-* farm parishes. But these parishes number only 26 out
of the 167 in Iceland, according to the tax list of 1847. Now I do not
hesitate to assert, with Guthbrand Vigfússon,[33] that "wherever in
Iceland farms have names with *saur-* there in olden times sacrifices
were made to Frey and more worship was shown to him and Freyja than
elsewhere." It is especially obvious that in such farmsteads Freyja was
honored more than other godheads, at least by the women. Wherever
feminine divinities occupied a place of honor in the religious beliefs of
a people, there the social position of women was unusually high. I
pointed out above that from the number of *-stathir* farm names having
women's names as their first element we can infer a great deal about the
position of women in society; and there I compared the number of such
names occurring in the four parts of Iceland. Now we shall consider
how these same farm names with *-stathir* and a woman's name are

[32] *Heimskringla, Ynglinga saga*, Chapter 4.
[33] See above, p. 41, note 2.

distributed, on the one hand among the *saur-* farm parishes, and on the other, among the other parishes which have no *saur-* farms within their boundaries. And we find that the *-stathir* farms with men's names in *saur-* parishes number 132, those with women's names, 27, or 17 per cent. Whereas in other parishes the women *-stathir* farms are proportionally fewer by half, viz., 8.8 per cent. Let that suffice!

I maintain also that skaldic culture and the great amount of women's rights at one time were branches of the same stem of culture. Now we have the opportunity to test that claim thoroughly. We have tolerably good information about the homes and birthplaces of thirty-three court skalds. Fourteen of them lived outside of the parishes having *saur-* farms. Among them is Illugi Bryndælaskáld, though he is a native of the Parish of Kjós. The others are: Tind Hallkelsson and Gunnlaug ormstunga, both of the Parish of Hvítarsítha, Skúli Thorsteinsson of the Parish of Borg, Glúm Geirason of the Parish of Skútustathir, Valgarth á Velli of the Parish of Hvól, Sigvat Thórtharson of the Parish of Grímsness, Hrafn Ǫnundarson of the Mosfell District, Thórth Kolbeinsson and his son Arnór of the Parish of Kolbeinsstathir, Thormóth Kolbrúnarskáld of Ǫgur Parish, Hrafn Guthrúnarson of Bæjar Parish, Bjarni Hallbjarnarson of Skefilsstathir Parish and Vigfús Víga-Glúmsson of Ǫngulsstathir Parish. Eight of the above mentioned lived in sections contiguous to *saur-* farm settlements. In these two groups of parishes and in those *saur-* farm parishes which boast of court skalds, there are 155 men- and women-*stathir* farms. Of these again, 19.4 per cent are *-stathir* farms bearing women's names, as against 8.2 per cent elsewhere. By itself, all this clearly points to the connection of *saur-* farms, skaldic skill, and the origin of the larger *-stathir* farms bearing women's names.

In the parishes with *saur-* farms the following skalds had their homes: Hofgartha-Ref and very likely also his foster son, Gissur gullbrárskáld, in Stathar Parish; Kormák and Bersi Skáld-Torfuson in Torfustathir Parish; Hallfreth vandræthaskáld in Ás Parish; Thorvald Hjaltason in Hóla Parish; Kolgrím the Little and Sneglu-Halli in Holt Parish; Thorleif Rauthfeldarson, Bolverk, and Thjóthólf, both sons of Arnór, in Svarfathardale Parish; Eilíf Guthrúnarson in Saurbær Parish; Skafti Thóroddsson and his son Stein in Ǫlfus Parish. In addition to these fourteen court skalds, the following (also court skalds) had kinsmen in *saur-* farm parishes: Einar skálaglamm, Stúf the Blind, Stein Herdísarson, Kálf Mánason, and Thórarin Skeggjason. Their own homes are not known, but when we note the homesteads of the nearest of their forebears, Einar, Stein, and Stúf belong to the Helgafell District; Kálf to the Vindhæli Parish; and Thórarin to the Villingaholt Parish. Thus nineteen court skalds would hail (additionally) from *saur-* farm parishes. Taking into account the total number of parishes, we would have expected only five court skalds there, whereas they number thirty-three in the *saur-* farm parishes. So we can readily see in what sort of environment the Old Norse skaldic culture had its development: *It came to Iceland with the fertility worshippers who venerated female divinities.*

# 3. Skalds, "Easterners," -AR Names

Among the most striking characteristics of Old Icelandic culture are skaldship and the great independence of women. Both of these traits were seen to be closely associated with the worship of fertility, and both followed the same course of development, being the inheritance of generations that never saw our country. We may be certain that the main areas of the primitive Norse worship of fertility were Denmark and Sweden. Indeed, there are cogent reasons for calling it an East Scandinavian creed, and it is important to bear this in mind when reflecting on the information given us by that versatile genius Snorri Sturluson about the origin of skaldship in the Northlands. According to him the skill in this craft is supposed to have been brought there by Ása-Óthin and his followers. His accounts about the "songsmiths," as he calls them, are tied to East Scandinavia exclusively. This is remarkable when we consider that Iceland, the chief land of Norse skaldic culture, was not colonized from Denmark or Sweden but rather from Norway. It is therefore most likely that memories were kept alive of the coming to Denmark and Sweden of a tribe that carried with it the culture which, centuries later, more notably shaped the intellectual life of the Icelanders than that of any other people in the world. Also, there are extant ancient accounts of the immigration to Norway of East Scandinavians previous to the discovery and colonization of Iceland. If we attach any importance to these accounts, it should not surprise us if the cultural inheritance of these "songsmiths" underwent an exceptional development in our country. Examples from the history of mankind of tribes removing themselves from one land to another are not rare. As the matter has not been investigated, who knows whether this might not have happened in the history of the colonization of Iceland. It is important for anyone who wishes to investigate the origin of skaldic culture in Iceland to bear this possibility in mind.

The accounts of the immigration of East Scandinavian people into Norway cannot be unraveled exhaustively without difficulty. As so often is the case with archaeological investigations, the path to the goal is crooked and thorny. Of course the most direct approach would be to scrutinize the distinctive culture and origin of each of the old families producing skalds, but there is no opportunity to do so at this time. It will be sufficient here to expatiate on the skalds of the Eastland, their families and their cultural environment. This field of research is fairly well marked out. In Finnur Jónsson's large collection of skaldic poetry[1] there are stanzas or ditties by six skalds of the Eastland who flourished during the tenth and eleventh centuries, and to them we shall now direct our attention. They are Hallstein Thengilsson of Hofthi in the Hofthi Settlement; Thórir snepil, who took land at Lund in Fnjóskadale; Glúm Geirason of Geirastathir by Lake Mývatn; Grím Droplaugarson of Arneitharstathir in Fljótsdale; Helgi Ásbjarnarson, who last lived at Eith; and Tjorvi the Scoffer, of Skaptfell.

About the skald Hallstein Thengilsson we know only that he composed these lines when learning of the death of his father: "Droops Hofthi [a promontory], death took Thengil; smile the slopes, seeing Hallstein." His deceased father had the sobriquet "the much sailing one," just like Thránd Bjarnarson. In Thrándarholt, Thengil, the uncle of Helgi the Lean, "took possession of land with the consent of Helgi." These two particulars in that very brief anecdote in the Book of Settlements,[2] when taken together, indicate with some probability that Thengil was somehow closely connected with that Gautish family of skalds (Helgi) in the Eyjafjord, or else had grown up in the same tract, though he came to Iceland from Hálogaland (Norway), and Helgi the Lean, from the Hebrides. Our sources unfortunately permit us no other

[1] *Den norsk-islandske Skjaldedigtning* (Copenhagen, 1912–1915).
[2] *Ldn.* § 185.

observations about the two kinsmen from Hofthi, Hallstein and Thengil.

We are in a somewhat better position with regard to the family and origins of Thórir snepil. He is said to be descended from the Hrafnista (Norway) family on the sword side. He and Án Redcloak are the only ones among the settlers who claim that origin. According to the Book of Settlements both share the characteristics which group them with Helgi the Lean, Ingimund the Old, and Gnúpa-Bárth. Án Redcloak and Greloth, his wife, during their first year in Iceland dwelled in Dufansdale. "It seemed to Greloth that an ill stench came out of the ground there," and for that reason Án moved to other quarters. "There to Greloth the fragrance of honey seemed to rise from the herbage."[3] Thórir snepil took possession of Kaldakinn (Cold Cheek) Promontory between Skuggaberg and the Ljósavatn Gap. He did not like it there and moved away. On that occasion he spoke this verse:

> Here lieth, keel-urger,
> Kaldakinn from of old;
> but hale we journeyed,
> helm-wielder, away thence.[4]

Thórir burns his fingers on the same hot iron as do Helgi, Ingimund, and Gnúpa-Bárth. He is forewarned no more than they of the sea wind. The "Cheek" of which he took possession, to start with, proved indeed to be a cold Cheek; still, he escaped "hale" from there, together with Hjálmun-Gaut, and sought shelter in the woods of Fnjóskadale. There at Lund (Grove) he built his farm and "worshipped the grǫve with sacrifice." Like Ingimund and Helgi, Thórir appears to be of East Scandinavian origin: In the Hauksbók version of the Book of Settlements the following is told about his mother: "Ketil brimil married Jórunn, the daughter of Thorgný the Lawman from Sweden."[5]

[3] *Ldn.* § 184.
[4] *Ldn.* § 284.
[5] *Ldn.* § 284.

Thórir snepil and Gnúpa-Bárth have more in common than their flight from the sea wind. Both name their farms Lund. Bárth at first lives at Lundarbrekka (L. Slope), and it is quickly evident that this farm name has the same significance, culturally, as the Lund in Fnjóskadale. Geiri, the grandson of Bárth, lived at Lund in the Fljót District. In this later landtake of Gnúpa-Bárth there also was in olden times a farm named Lund—and in Catholic times a church was located there. In addition to the two Lund farms we have mentioned, Finnur Jónsson in his work on farm names[6] enumerates a Lund in Holt Parish, a Lund in Thverárhlíth Parish, and Lund in Lundarreykjadale. The latter farm has been a churchstead since olden times. Other old farms with this name are not known. Lund in Holt Parish lies close by Knappstathir, the homestead of the settler Thórth knapp. Like Thormóth the Strong of Sigluness, Thórth knapp in the Hauksbók version of the Book of Settlements is spoken of in plain words as Swedish.[7] A short distance from Lund in the Thverárhlíth Parish was the farm of Hrómund, the foster brother of Ingimund the Old; and at Lund in the Lundarreykjadale there lived in heathen times the descendants of Grím of Hálogaland. He was a brother of Hrómund and likewise a foster brother of Ingimund. From Grím was descended Thorlaug the Priestess, wife of Oddi Ýrarson. She is reported to have been the sister of Kjallak Hrólfsson of Lund. At the same time we shall call to mind that in the section of the story about Geirmund heljarskinn we read that the people of Skarth, kinsmen of Oddi, in the olden times worshipped a certain rowan tree grove at Skarth.[8] We do not need to say more about the farm at Lund. All these farms appear to be centered around the places where the fertility worship and East Scandinavian influences might be expected to prevail in rich measure. Evidently more settlers than only Thórir snepil "worshipped groves."

Next we shall advert to Glúm Geirason. He is the only court skald

[6] *Safn til Sögu Íslands* (Copenhagen, 1907–1915), IV, 412–584.
[7] *Ldn.* § 258.
[8] *Geirmundar tháttr heljarskinns*, Chapter 6.

who can in any way be counted among Eastland skalds. He is the author of seventeen of the twenty-six stanzas from the tenth and eleventh centuries which the Eastland can claim in Finnur Jónsson's large collection of skaldic poetry. Doubtless Glúm's verse was not preserved or even known there. In the Reykdæla saga Geiri, Glúm's father, is called *austmathr* (Easterner),[9] a most peculiar name for a settler in Iceland. Geiri has only two namesakes there in heathen times whom we know of, viz., Geiri, the grandson of Gnúpa-Bárth, whom we mentioned before; and Geiri, the son of Geirdís in Holt, who most likely was a kinswoman of the settler Frithleif the Gautish at Holt. From the time of the Settlement only one other man is known to have had the surname of *austmathr*, viz., Eyvind austmathr, the father of Helgi the Lean and half brother of Thránd the Much Sailing. "Eyvind was called *austmathr* because he came west over the sea from Sweden," as the Hauksbók version has it.[10] This explanation is no doubt correct. At the same time, we have to take into account that it would fit settler Geiri as well. From this infrequent surname it would perhaps be easy to draw the conclusion that the participation in the settlement of Iceland of persons who came directly from Sweden was slight. But this is not the same as saying that the share of East Scandinavians was small. Consider the surname of Uni the Dane. He was descended from a Swedish family, like Eyvind the "Easterner," but his father "had landed possessions in Seeland." There Uni was brought up, and so he received the surname of "the Dane," even though he was of Swedish origin. The same is true of the brothers Ketil and Thormóth, the sons of Bresi (Bersi), who took possession of land on Akraness. They must have had the same forebears on their father's side as Ingimund the Old, and they are stated to be from the eastern Baltic. Yet in the Hauksbók version these brothers are called Irish: They came to Iceland after a long sojourn in Ireland, or else they were brought up among the Irish. Examples like these indicate clearly on how exceedingly uncertain and unsafe a basis rests the doctrine of

9 *Reykdæla saga*, Chapter 17.
10 *Ldn.* § 40.

the Norwegian origin of the Icelanders. Even though the majority of our forefathers who settled here did come from Norway, that does not prove that they were of West Scandinavian origin. On the other hand, we have here the explanation why the people of Iceland have been termed a branch of the Norwegian stock.

We must not part with the "Easterners" Eyvind and Geiri, the father of the skald Glúm, without recalling the "Easterners" whom Thorbjorn hornklofi mentions in his Lay of Harald. That poem is regarded as having been composed shortly after the Battle in the Hafrsfjord. In it Harald Fairhair is called "the king of the Norwegians" and "the sole ruler of the Eastmen."[11] There is no question but that the designation Norwegians is here used for all the inhabitants of Norway. Also, we learn from the poem Ynglingatal (Enumeration of the Ynglings) of Thjóthólf of Hvin and from the narrative of Ohthere (Óttar) of Hálogaland, who stayed with Alfred the Great, King of England, toward the end of the ninth century, that the names "Norway" and "Norwegians" at that time had nearly the same meaning as nowadays. If so, then what is the significance of "Easterner" in Hornklofi's language? It is generally known that the Icelanders of the twelfth and thirteenth centuries called the Norwegians "Easterners," but this usage no doubt arose only in Iceland. Now just as they applied that term to Norwegians, the Norwegians in olden times called their neighbors east of the Keel by this name, or even all those peoples who lived in the Baltic lands. We know that the Celts in the British Islands called Westerners those who in the early times came to Iceland from Norway. On the other hand, the Scandinavian settlers in the lands west of the North Sea were not called so. It is therefore wholly improbable to assume that the Norwegians were in Hornklofi's time divided into "Easterners" or "Westerners" according to their place of residence. If that had been the usage in Norway at the time of the colonization, one would expect to encounter it also in Iceland, and that all the more so as the nation was for political purposes divided into Quarters called after the main points of

[11] *Haraldskvæthi*, stanzas 5 and 9.

the compass. However, in Iceland we hear of no "Easterners" or "Westerners," but only of Eastfirthings and Westfirthings.

It has been claimed that in Hornklofi's Lay of Harald a feeling of Norwegian nationalism could be detected. That certainly is not so. The words of the poet about King Harald's spouses preclude that. With obvious pride he states that the king had "rejected the maidens from Rogaland and Horthaland and every one from Heithmork and Hálogaland," and "had chosen the Danish woman."[12] The Danish woman no doubt is Ragnhild, of whom mention is made in the poem. Hornklofi says that the haughty *dísir* (here, maidens) of hers had other matters to talk about than that Harald did not feed the wolves on blood, when their own men did that. These remarks cannot be interpreted as betokening a feeling of Norwegian nationalism, though they do show some sentiment of antipathy toward Ragnhild's environment. From the connection one may infer that Ragnhild had been one of King Harald's antagonists. Besides, the expression of "feeding the wolves" most likely refers to Harald's victory in the Battle in the Hafrsfjord. The lines of Hornklofi about the Danish queen, or princess, and her "haughty *dísir*" rather suggests that the opponents of Harald in his struggle to bring Norway under his dominion may have been of East Scandinavian descent—as indeed King Harald himself was, as is well known. And we need not be surprised that "the Danish woman" had been one of his opponents: At the beginning of the Viking Age, or more precisely, before 813, Danish kings had achieved a foothold in South Norway and subdued West Fold, the wealthiest and most important part of Norway in those days. During the following generations viking bands from Denmark and Sweden obtained sway over the chief routes of commerce in West and East Europe and at the same time founded new colonies far and wide. It would indeed be astonishing if the coasts of Norway had been spared the visitations of these hosts. I refuse to believe that absurd notion.

Hornklofi calls King Harald's enemies in the Battle of the Hafrfjord

[12] *Ibid.*, stanza 14.

*austkylfur* (Men from the East with Clubs) and tells us that the King had given his men "Eastern maidens." At that time the incursions of vikings from Denmark and the coast lands of Norway in the lands west of the North Sea were at their height; and from the lay we can conclude, as Gustav Storm has pointed out,[13] that vikings from the British Islands had a hand in the battle against Harald Fairhair. For that reason one might imagine that Hornklofi had meant Western maidens rather than Eastern ones in the possession of Harald and his men after their victory. However, when we consider the word *austkylfur*, matters look different. It evidently signifies "Eastern Kylfings (club wielding men)," and it is the captured women of the vanquished Eastern antagonists whom the poet calls "Eastern maidens." In the Egils saga we hear about *Kylfings*. They came to Hálogaland from the East, and Thórolf Kveld-Úlfsson, the revenue officer of Harald Fairhair, came to blows with them. Gustav Storm was of the opinion that they were followers of the Swedish king, and that is not unlikely. Gartharíki (Russia) was founded by vikings from Sweden, and in the olden days this East Scandinavian colony was also called Kylfingaland. Now, according to Johannes Steenstrup[14] the club was the chief weapon of the Danish farmers and of still other Scandinavians in Viking times, whereas the Norwegians of those times clearly occupy a particular position in this matter: From the Viking Age alone some two thousand swords have been found in Norway. There, the sword must have belonged to the common equipment for warfare, whereas in Old Danish territory, on the other hand, very few swords have been found dating from that period, and only six in our country. So the following words in the Fóstbrœthra saga may deserve our attention: "At that time swords were infrequent for men's equipment in Iceland."[15] This instructive remark concerns men's arms in saga times. So now I hesitate no longer to assume the presence of East Scandinavian colonists in Norwegian coast lands at the time

[13] *Norsk historisk tidsskrift*, 2 række, Vol. II (1880), 325 f.

[14] *Normannerne* (Copenhagen, 1876), I, 236, 330 f.

[15] *Fóstbrœthra saga*, Chapter 3.

Harald Fairhair raised himself to power there. Hornklofi is likely to refer to the inhabitants of these coast lands when he calls his king the sovereign of the Easterners.

It may now be easier to discuss the extraction of the fourth skald of the Eastland, Grím Droplaugarson. The Book of Settlements informs us that his family was descended from Thórir Thithrandi, who in all likelihood had his home in Veradale east of the Throndheimsfjord in Norway. His sons, Ketil thrym and Graut-Atli, must have come to Iceland from there. They took possession of both sides of Lake Lagar-fljót; and Grím belonged to the third generation descended from Ketil thrym, and wholly on the sword side. Ketil thrym has two namesakes in the old sagas. One of them was Ketil thrym in Njarthvík, his grand-son. We are told about him in the story entitled "How Norway Was Settled";[16] and this Ketil thrym must in times of yore have lived at Thruma in the District of Agthir (Norway), because he is said to be one of the fourth generation descended from Nór, a king in the East Baltic, who is said to have conquered Norway. In the same breath, after this King Thrym is mentioned in the line descended from King Nór, we also hear of Végarth, "the father of Vethrorm, the father of Vémund the Old." These names at once direct our thoughts to the account in the Book of Settlements of Ketil thrym, the grandfather of Grím Drop-laugarson. There[17] we are told that "Ketil went abroad and stayed with Véthorm, the son of Vémund the Old." In the Droplaugarsona saga more details are given about this journey abroad, and Véthorm is there called Vethrorm. In these accounts we encounter the same names, viz., Ketil thrym, Vethrorm, and Vémund the Old. These names are al-together too rare to allow of the possibility of coincidence. Nowhere is there mention of any kinship between the friends of Vethrorm, the son of Vémund, and Ketil thrym, the settler; but it is obvious that at one time their families must have been linked up with that of Ketil thrym in Thruma and Vémund the Old, the son of Vethrorm. The agreement of

---

[16] *Hversu Noregr byggthist*, Chapter I.
[17] *Ldn.* § 324.

the line descended from Nór and the accounts about Ketil thrym show
that this was the case.

In the story "How Norway Was Settled" only one line is traced
from King Nór down to the settlers of Iceland, viz., to the two brothers
on Akraness who were the sons of Bresi. It comes to an end with
Tungu-Odd, the son of Thormóth's daughter. This exception is
singular; but the fact is that in the thirteenth century the people of
Reykholt administered Tungu-Odd's *gothi*dom, used his home pastures,
and were descended from him. As to other settlers in Iceland who
claimed Nór as their forebear, the author of the story contents himself
with tracing them down to Ketil thrym in Thruma, Vémund the Old,
Ketil raum, and King Hjorleif the Uxorious. In the Book of Settlements Geirmund heljarskinn is reckoned to belong to the third generation from Hjorleif on the sword side, and Ingimund the Old to the
second, from Ketil raum. Now, one may say that relatives are apt to
resemble one another: The families enumerated which claim to be
descended from King Nór evince among themselves unusually distinct
characteristics of East Scandinavian culture.

Here then we have five family branches all of which must have
sprung from the same East Scandinavian root. One may shrug one's
shoulders about the historical learning which speaks of an East Scandinavian root in connection with that unhistorical figure of King Nór.
But let us see! There are known from the ninth and tenth centuries
some men's names which have -*orm* as their second element. They are,
according to E. H. Lind's book of names,[18] Hallorm, Ketilorm,
Ráthorm, Vethrorm, and Thórorm. It is instructive to consider where
they occur. Hallorm is the name of the son-in-law of Ingimund the Old,
who lived in Vatnsdale. Close by Atlavík, the homestead of Graut-Atli,
the brother of Ketil thrym, lies the farm of Hallormsstath. No other
Hallorm is known in Iceland, but there is one in Norway dating from
about 1400. Ketilorm is the name of a man who figures in the Drop-

[18] E. H. Lind, *Norsk-isländska dopnamn och fingerade namn från medeltiden*
(Uppsala, 1905–1915), *sub verbo*.

laugarsona saga.[19] He lived by Lake Lagarfljót, as did the Hallorm after whom the farm Hallormsstath is named. Vethrorm Vémundarson, the friend of Ketil thrym, also is the only one of that name. He lived east in Jamtaland (Sweden), and Ketil visited him there. There are another three who bear the name of Thórorm, and they are easy to locate. One lived at Thruma in the District of Agthir (Norway), the old home of the oldest Ketil thrym; the second, in Thórormstunga in Vatnsdale. He was the brother of Hallorm, the son-in-law of Ingimund. And the third was the son of Tungu-Odd's daughter and lived at Rauthamel. Finally, there is one Ráthorm, a settler who lived in Vetleifsholt. He was the brother of Jólgeir. Because of their names, Lind considers the last two to have been East Scandinavians. In addition to those named above, Lind adduces the following -*orm* names from Norway. There is a farm in the Veradale called Landormsstathir. From this neighborhood came Ketil thrym and Graut-Atli. Two men with the name of Lindorm are known from the end of the Middle Ages, one in Hálogaland, the other in Jamtaland. Lind is of the opinion that the name Lindorm is "borrowed" from Sweden. I consider it safe to say that about the whole group of -*orm* names. They hardly struck root in Norway and appear to be connected with the small number of settlers whose line was traced to King Nór from the East Baltic.

The conception of the emigration of men from the Baltic to Norway under the leadership of Nór will be our next consideration. It is the main thread in the story of "How Norway Was Settled." In a few Icelandic families there lived the memory of their ultimately East Scandinavian origin, straight counter to the general, and indeed to some extent natural, view of historians that our people were of Norwegian stock. The author of this story assumes the purely East Scandinavian colonization of Norway. And now let us call to mind the expressions used by Hornklofi: "sovereign of the Easterners," "Eastern Club Wielding Men," and "Eastern maidens." But, of course, the author of our story has this settlement, or establishment of a colony, by

[19] *Droplaugarsona saga*, Chapters 13 f.

the Easterners, take place long before the beginning of the settlement of Iceland. He had before him rigmaroles of genealogies reaching far back into ancient times. With their first generation he points to the arrival in Norway of the men from the Baltic, and links that line with members of his own invention, but how much of the genealogies in his story is pure fiction is hard to determine. Still, the *-orm* names in them tend to show that the old idea of an East Scandinavian conquest in Norway is not just a wild guess.

Now it is, to be sure, true that no *-orm* names occur in the lineage of Geirmund heljarskinn or in his neighborhood. But that does not matter much, because weighty considerations assign to his family a place with that of Ingimund the Old, Ketil thrym, the sons of Bersi, and Vémund the Old. Oddi Ýrarson was the son of Geirmund's daughter; Galti Kjalvararson, the son of Thormóth Bersason's daughter; and the farm of Kjalvararstathir was named after Kjalvara. Grím Droplaugarson belonged to the third generation descended from Ketil thrym, and Grím named the farm of Arneitharstathir after his wife. Hardly anywhere in our land are there, proportionally, found so many *-stathir* farms with a woman's name as the first element as in the vicinity of Ingimund the Old and of the brothers, Ketil thrym and Graut-Atli. And where else in our land would we expect to find as many women priests and sacerdotesses as in these same families, and thus also in the line of Bjorn buna? That family too apparently traced its origin to people from the Baltic, because Bjorn's wife must have been Vélaug, the sister of Vémund the Old. And there are five priestesses to be found in these families: Frithgerth in Hvamm in the Dales District, who was the wife of Thórarin fylsenni; "Thuríth, the temple priestess," who belongs to the family of the Freysgythlings; Thórlaug, the wife of Oddi Ýrarson; Thuríth, the daughter-in-law of Ingimund the Old; and Steinvor, who in the Vápnfirthinga saga is called a kinswoman of Brodd-Helgi. "She was a temple priestess and the custodian of the main sanctuary," as the author of the saga puts it.[20] By comparing the sources

[20] *Vápnfirthinga saga*, Chapter 3.

we can ascertain that this main sanctuary was located on the land owned by the family of Graut-Atli; and Brodd-Helgi was the son of Ásvor, daughter of Thórir, the son of Graut-Atli. Very likely Steinvor was her sister. She took upon herself the care of the temple, since Einar, the son of Graut-Atli, had died when still young. At the beginning of the eleventh century Sorli, the son of Brodd-Helgi, was the *gothi* of the Fljótsdale District and lived at Valthjófsstath. Contemporary with him were the *gothar* in the Múlathing District, viz., Sithu-Hall at Thvottá; Hrafnkel the Priest at Hrafnkelsstathir; Holmstein, the son of Spak-Bersi at Bersastathir; Ketil thrym the Younger at Njarthvík; and Bjarni, the son of Brodd-Helgi, at Hof in the Vápnafjord. All these men were descendants on the sword side of the five landtakers who, together with Graut-Atli, are called in the postscript of the Hauksbók version the most eminent in the Múlathing District. According to the laws of the land, six *gothi*doms were to exist there, and one chief sanctuary for each one. All these *gothi*doms, barring only that of Graut-Atli, were maintained beyond the time of the Conversion, in the direct male line of these families. It is clear now why Steinvor the Priestess besought the help of her kinsman, Brodd-Helgi, in the prosecution of the case against Thorleif the Christian, as is told in the Vápnfirthinga saga:[21] The male line of her family had died out.

Evident as it is that Grím Droplaugarson belonged to a family of fertility worshippers, this is even clearer in the case of the fifth skald of Eastland, Helgi Ásbjarnarson. His grandfather was Hrafnkel Freysgothi, who lost a boar in Skrithdale and had such love for Frey that he gave him "half of his most treasured possessions."[22] One stanza is attributed to Helgi Ásbjarnarson. It is a difficult one to interpret, yet so much is clear that the skald sought at night to obtain an omen from the trees of his forest. About the occasion of this stanza the author of the Drop-laugarsona saga has this to say:[23] "Now Helgi Ásbjarnarson bought the parcel of land called Eithar, which is outlying in the district, and sold

[21] *Ibid.*, Chapter 5.   [22] *Hrafnkels saga Freysgotha*, Chapter 2.
[23] *Droplaugarsona saga*, Chapters 12 and 13.

Mjóvaness. He thought that an advantageous purchase because his thingmen dwelled round about there. He had a locked bed-closet made [in his house]. Thordís, his wife, asked him why he wanted to own land there where the woods grew up to the farm and one could not see people going or coming, even though they approached the farmhouse. Then Helgi spoke a stanza." The verse he speaks is in answer to Thordís' question, hence one should think it furnished a hint as to why Helgi moved to Eithar. And that appears to be the case. At Eithar there was a grove in which sacrifices were performed. Tormented by fear of Grím Droplaugarson's plans for bringing about his death, and of his ambushes to avenge his brother Helgi's death, Helgi Ásbjarnarson seeks the protection and the warning signs of the powers in the sacred grove. Adam of Bremen reports[24] that at Uppsala there was a grove in which were hung the carcasses of animals sacrificed, which information he had from an eyewitness. This grove is so sacred in the eyes of the heathens, says Adam, that every separate tree is regarded as divine because of the animals sacrificed and their putrefaction. Somewhat similar was Thórir snepil's grove and the trees by the farm at Eithar from which Helgi Ásbjarnarson sought enlightenment about his fate.

It is clear from the evidence that the accounts of Frey worship in the Eastland are all interwoven in the account of Hrafnkel Freysgothi and his grandson Helgi. In the Northland they appear exclusively in the Vatnsdæla saga and the Víga-Glúms saga, and especially the accounts which deal with the descendants of Ingimund the Old and Helgi the Lean. This is, of course, not accidental. These sagas have to do with three Freysgothi families. In the main the cultural milieu of all these families is the same. It is for this reason that the choice of subject matter in traditions concerning them is so closely similar. Hrafnkel loves his horse Freyfaxi, and for it undergoes the worst tribulations. This horse historically has only one name in the old literature. It is mentioned in the Vatnsdæla saga, and reports about it warn the sons of Ingimund:[25]

[24] Adamus Bremensis, *Historia Hammaburgensis Ecclesiæ*, Book IV, § 27.
[25] *Vatnsdæla saga*, Chapter 34.

"Brand owned a stallion with a mane differing in color from his body, named Freyfaxi. He was careful about this horse because he considered it valuable. It could be depended on, both for horse fighting and otherwise; and most people considered it true that Brand believed in Faxi." —"Hrafnkel had this treasured possession which he valued above all other things. It was a stallion, of iron gray color, with a black stripe along his backbone, which he called Freyfaxi. He gave half of this horse to his friend Frey. His love for this horse was so great that he made the vow that he would slay any one who rode him without his permission."[26] The essence of both these passages as well as the mention of the coloring is virtually the same.

Both Helgi Ásbjarnarson and Víga-Glúm evict their tenants from their farms. The account about Helgi's procedure is found in the Brandkrossa *tháttr* (short story);[27] that of Víga-Glúm, in his saga:[28] "Helgi established his farm at Oddsstathir, and planned to transfer his household and possessions thither in one day, the first of the 'moving days' (four successive days at the end of May). But when Odd, (Helgi's tenant) made ready to depart he had a bull slaughtered and roasted; and on the first of the 'moving days,' when ready to depart, he had the table set and benches placed the full length of the hall, and all the meat from the steer was dished up on the table. Odd went up to it and spoke as follows: 'Now here is the table set carefully as for the dearest friends of mine. This banquet I dedicate altogether to Frey, so that he may let him who comes in my stead depart from Oddsstathir with no less regret than I depart now.' Thereupon Odd left the place with all his belongings." And now about the departure of Thorkel the Tall from Thverá: "Before Thorkel departed from Thverá he went to the sanctuary of Frey, leading an old ox up to it, and said: 'Freyr,' he said, 'you who have been the one in whom I put full confidence and have received many gifts from me and have repaid them fully,—now I give

26 *Hrafnkels saga Freysgotha*, Chapter 3.
27 *Brandkrossa tháttr*, Chapter 1.
28 *Víga-Glúms saga*, Chapter 9

you this ox, so that Glúm may leave Thverá farm not less unwilling than I do now. And let me see some signs whether or not you will accept this gift.' And the ox bellowed at that and dropped down dead."

I shall have to let these two parallel passages suffice for the present, though more could be adduced. Both are the only ones of the kind in the old literature. No doubt their similarity could be explained in different ways; but however explained, it will be difficult to get around the fact that in regard to their spiritual attitude the family of Helgi Ásbjarnarson is intimately related to the Gautish skald families in the Eyjafjord District and the Vatnsdale. We can now understand better that it is not an insignificant coincidence that tales about swine are attached to the names of Helgi, Ingimund, and Hrafnkel, and that it is not just accidentally that the authors of the Hrafnkels saga and the Vatndæla saga make use of the expression "it seemed as though two heads were on each animal" when speaking about the livestock of Ingimund and Hrafnkel. Behind these strange words lies hidden a meaning which seems so admirably befitting the worshippers of Frey and fertility.

Our sources do not agree as to whether the skald Tjorvi the Scoffer from the Skaptfell District was the son of a sister or the son of Hróar Tungugothi, but they are agreed as to Hróar's paternity. He is declared to be the son of Uni the Dane, the son of Garthar, the son of Svavar the Swede. Birger Nerman has called attention to the fact that men's names ending in *-ar* are in general older and far more common among East Scandinavians than among West Scandinavians.[29] He has adduced very strong arguments to support his thesis. Among his examples he mentions the *-ar* names that so strongly characterize the line of Uni the Dane: Svavar, Garthar, Hróar, and, we may add, Gunnar, which was the name of the brother of Tjorvi the Scoffer. There are also other names that tend to indicate that Uni was rightly considered an East

[29] Birger Nerman, *Studier över Svärges hedna literatur* (Uppsala, 1913), pp. 51–66. Note the distinction between the masculine suffix *-ar* (r) (mostly from* *-harjar*) in names, and the genitive singular ending *-ar*.

Scandinavian. In but few places in our land is there found such a collection of strange names from the olden times as in the tract of which he took possession, the present parishes of Eithathinghá and Hjaltastathathinghá. In these two parishes there are, according to Jón Jónsson's register of farms, fifteen with -*stathir* as second element and a man's name as the first. Among them occur the names Áni, Bóndi, Hrollaug, Kórek, Tóki, and Vithar. In addition, the Droplaugarsona saga testifies to there having lived men there with such names as Igul, Ketilorm, and Oddmar. These very infrequent names rather point to the fact that many of the settlers in Uni's landtake were East Scandinavians. Nor is it less noteworthy to encounter the farm name Hleithrar (or Hleithar)garth in the landtake of a man from Seeland. That was what Icelanders called the capital, famed of old, of the Seeland kings. In later times Hleithrargarth in Eithathinghá parish was called Hleinagarth, but old deeds put the matter beyond doubt what was the original name. There is one other farm of this name in our land, viz., Hleithrargarth in the Eyjafjord District. There, toward the end of the Period of Settlement or a little later, lived Thorkel the Swart, the son of Thórir snepil, and his wife, Guthlaug, the daughter of a son of Helgi the Lean. The line of Guthlaug is traced back to prehistoric Danish kings, and near kinsmen of hers bore the same names as these kings: Her father's name was Hrólf, her uncle's, Ingjald, and their father was called Helgi. In this line there lived stories about the old kings in Hleithrar; and therefore the reports are correct that Helgi the Lean traced his ancestry not only to Gautland, but also to Seeland. So it is clear why the two Hleithrargarth names occur precisely in his landtake and in that of Uni the Dane.

There are two farms in Uni's landtake called Rauthholt (Red Woods) and Snjóholt (Snow Woods). These names arrested my attention when I leafed through the farm register of 1847. The facts of the case are as follows: Among the one thousand farms there mentioned as existing on the tract of land from Laugaland on the Eyjafjord to the Jokulsá River in the Lón District there are only three -*holt* farms, whereas among one thousand farms between the Jokulsá River on the Sólheim Strands and the Thurá River in the Olfus District there are seventy-two or more. That is rather strange. To be sure, we must take into account that the physical nature and the vegetation of the land had a substantial influence in the naming of farms with -*holt* (woods or rough stony ridge) as their second element. Nevertheless, the difference between these tracts in this respect is so insignificant that it became necessary to look for other explanations. I remembered a passage which preserved some East Scandinavian heathendom. It is found in the Guta saga and runs as follows:[30] "Before that time, and long thereafter, people worshipped woods and hills, sanctuaries, sacred premises, and heathen divinities." A similar definition is found also in West Scandinavian heathendom, in the so-called Christian Laws of King Sverri: "We must not do sacrifice to heathen wights, nor to heathen gods, nor to hills or heathen stone altars."[31] Here the worship of woods is not mentioned. Nor was this to be expected, for the most learned scholars consider this sentence lifted from the old Gulathing Laws. In the regions where these laws were in force -*holt* farms are remarkably rare. They are, on the other hand, exceedingly widespread in Sweden, and especially in West Gautland, Småland, and Halland, which provinces in the olden times belonged to Denmark. Historically we know of some two hundred farm names in -*holt* in Iceland.

In the Book of Settlements and the Vatnsdæla saga, both of which are so peculiarly rich in memories of East Scandinavian culture, there are found traditions which afford us clear clues as to how to regard farm names in -*holt* as used in heathen times. The wisewoman Heith predicts for Ingimund and his foster brothers Hrómund and Grím that they would "dwell in the land west in the ocean which was as yet undiscovered; but Ingimund said that he would prevent that coming about. The wisewoman said he would not be able to do that, and that it would serve as a token of her speaking the truth that a certain thing [or figure]

---

[30] *Guta Lag och Guta Saga, sub "af blotan."*
[31] *Norges gamle Love* (Christiania, 1846), I, 337.

would disappear from out of his pouch, and that he would find it again when digging [the foundations] for his high-seat pillars."[32] Ingimund liked it nowhere. Therefore King Harald urged him to seek his destiny in Iceland, but Ingimund declared that he did not intend to do that. Yet he sent two Finns to travel to Iceland in the shape of animals to find the figure he had lost. That was an image of Frey made of silver. The Finns returned and reported they had found the figure but had not been able to get hold of it. They pointed out to him a valley between three groves and told him about the nature of the land and the location where they were to dwell. Thereafter Ingimund sailed to Iceland. "During the winter Ingimund lived in the Vithidale grove. From there they saw in the south mountains not covered with snow, and journeyed thither in spring. There Ingimund recognized the lands to which he had been directed. His daughter Thórdís was born in Thórdís Woods."[33]

For the Frey worshipper Ingimund the Old it was, to be sure, no new thing that a hillock or an elevation overgrown with woods was to be his homestead. Such spots our heathen forebears called a *holt* (stony hill). Frey had decided that Ingimund was to live by a *holt*, and so he does. In fact, he twice chooses a place of residence by a *holt* before finding the image of Frey in the hill, as is indicated by the names Ingimundarholt and Thórdísarholt. Ingimund worships holy trees, as did the people by the Baltic, and like the skalds Thórir snepil and Helgi Ásbjarnarson. This makes it clearer than before why *-lund* (grove) farms abound in the districts above mentioned. The same is true about the *-holt* farms established in heathen times: They were set up by people with an East Scandinavian culture. In the Book of Settlements some thirty *-holt* farms are mentioned. Not one of them is found in the Northeastland. We first encounter the name of Holt in the farm of the settler Frithleif from Gautland, then in Ingimundarholt and Thórdísarholt. Then there is the farm Hjartharholt in the Dales District which, according to the author of Laxdæla saga, was established by Ólaf the

[32] *Vatnsdæla saga*, Chapter 10.
[33] *Ibid.*, Chapter 15.

Peacock. His father Hoskuld had a host of kinsfolk in Denmark, as related in the same saga. Bjorn the Easterner, the grandson of Bjorn buna and son-in-law of the East Scandinavian warrior king Ólaf the White, established himself at Borgarholt in Bjarnar Harbor. Gerth, his son's daughter, was the mother of Guthlaug the Rich at Borgarholt in the Miklaholt District. He was the son-in-law of Thuríth, the daughter of Tungu-Odd, who had dwelled at Horgarholt in the same district. Close by lies Reykholt. Thither, so the Book of Settlements tells us, Tungu-Odd went from his house to bathe (in the hot pool there).[34] The farm of Jorund the Christian, the son of Ketil, his maternal uncle from Akraness, was called Jorundarholt. At Thrándarholt there lived Thránd the Much Sailing, who was the brother of Eyvind the Easterner; and Ráthorm, the brother of Jólgeir, lived at Vetleifsholt. We may add that Ófeig grettir "lived at Ofeigsstathir near Steinsholt," Thormóth skafti at Skaftaholt, and Ozzur, the father of Thórth the Freys*gothi*, at Bakkarholt. The last-named three, as well as Bjorn the Easterner at Borgarholt, must belong to the male lineage of Vatnar Víkarsson. I have now enumerated half of the -*holt* farms mentioned in the Book of Settlements. It is no exaggeration, then, to say that these examples furnish an unmistakable indication of the cultural origin of the old farm names in -*holt*.

But we shall not remain in any uncertainty about this matter. That is not necessary. The observations of Birger Nerman concerning the names in -*ar*[35] will now stand us in good stead in an astonishing manner. The kin of Uni the Dane were marked by their -*ar* names, and his land-take, by its -*holt* farms. It is worth the trouble to observe whether these appellations went hand in hand in heathen times. The procedure for this investigation is clear. I counted the -*ar* names in the Book of Settlements occurring during the Settlement and the Saga Period and found their number to be about sixty. Then I considered how frequent such names were in the male line of persons who in the Book of Settlements

[34] *Ldn.* § 200.
[35] *Studier över Svärges hedna literatur* (Uppsala, 1913), pp. 51–66.

are said to be the occupants of *-holt* farms, and the result was as follows:

| FARM | OCCUPANT |
| --- | --- |
| Arnarholt | Thorbjorn, grandfather of Einar |
| Borgarholt | Bjorn, father of Óttar, grandfather of Einar |
| Brautarholt | Authun, fourth generation after Thjóstar |
| Bothvarsholt | |
| Gunnarsholt | Gunnar, grandfather of Gunnar |
| Holt | Frithleif, father of Thjóthar |
| Holt | Óleif, father of Vestar |
| Horgsholt | Thuríth, great granddaughter of Úlfar |
| Jorundarholt | Jorund, grandfather of Einar, the father of Hávar |
| Reykjaholt | Onund, the son of Úlfar |
| Skaftaholt | Thormóth, the grandson of Einar |
| Stafaholt | Teit, the father of Einar |
| Steinsholt | Ófeig, the son of Einar |
| Onundarholt | Onund, the son of Hróar |

This little list comprises nearly half of the *-holt* farms mentioned in the Book of Settlements and almost every fourth *-ar* name in it dating from the time of colonization and the Saga Period. It is hardly necessary to adduce at greater length testimony to the fact that these names go precisely with those lineages which were worshippers of groves. They are particularly frequent in the great families which produced skalds, and there is a notably strong showing of these names connected with skalds who bore metronymic names. This distinctive feature is particularly marked in the families of the skalds Eilíf Guthrúnarson, Eyjólf Valgertharson, Stein Herdísarson, and Thorgils Holluson. This entire clan is descended from King Vatnar Víkarsson. The grandfather of Herdís, the mother of Stein, was the skald Einar skálaglamm Helgason, who was the son of Óttar, who again was the son of Bjorn the Easterner. Eyjólf, the son of Valgerth, is also the son of Einar and the father of the skald Einar of Thverá. The brothers Bothvar and Vithar of Gnúpufell probably are the brothers of the grandfather of Eilíf Guthrúnarson. The

Eyfirthing clan all trace their line to Helgi the Lean and Thórunn hyrna, the sister of Bjorn the Easterner. Hrafn Guthrúnarson is reckoned to be the male cousin of the court skald Óttar the Swart. Both are called the sons of the sister of the skald Sighvat, who was the son of Thórth, the skald of Sigvaldi. Ólaf Bjargeyjarson was the son of a sister of Gunnar Valbrandsson; and Kormák Dolluson was the son of a sister of the skald Steiner Sjónason. Among the kinsmen of Grím Droplaugarson we find Einar Thórisson, the son of Graut-Atlason. We have not as yet mentioned Bersi Skáld-Torfuson and Volu-Stein. But we know little about the lineage of Volu-Stein, and of Bersi we know only his mother's name.

Thus the *-ar* names have proved themselves eminently useful. From their connection with the *-holt* farms it is evident that both customs of naming are of East Scandinavian origin. At the same time, they give a new indication in what direction the search should turn for seeking the origin of Icelandic skaldship. The absence of swords among our forebears in heathen times also gave some hints, which became rather significant when we recall Hornklofi's words about *austkylfur* (Men from the East with Clubs), Eastern maidens, and Easterners. Nor is it to be forgotten that it appears as though skaldship ebbed out in Norway at the time our land was being colonized. Those who remained in the East (Norway) continued to wear swords at their sides, whereas those who sailed west across the Atlantic—to Iceland—continued to compose poetry.

# 4. Skalds, Sacrifices to Frey, Antiquities

Ingimund the Old sends "two Finns in the shape of animals to Iceland after his figurine. That was [an image of] Frey, made of silver." The figure had vanished from his pouch at home in Norway. Einar skálaglamm from the Breithafjord accepted as a present two small images in human shape;[1] and Hallfreth vandræthaskáld was accused of having worshipped small images of that sort after being baptized.[2] No other reports of small images of gods or men are known from the literature. It is of little importance what these images were to signify, and the validity of the reports about them is merely corroborative. Certainly no one will believe that Ingimund's Frey image was carried by the winds from Hefni in Norway to the wooded ridge in the Vatnsdale where later he established his farm and erected a temple in honor of Frey. Likewise, it is most questionable, by all means, whether Hallfreth vandræthaskáld had at any time walked about with the image of a god in his pouch, or whether Einar skálaglamm had received images of this sort as a present. But when we take into account that both Ingimund and Hallfreth lived in Vatnsdale, it becomes rather probable that people in that vicinity knew about such pocket images of gods. Let us also at the same time note that the owners of such small images of whom we are told very probably were fertility worshippers. About Ingimund the Old no further testimony is needed in this regard. And from the verse of Hallfreth it appears likely that the Vanir gods were especially dear to him. When Hallfreth marries he settles in Gautland, the former homeland of his compatriots of the kin of Ingimund the

[1] It is, rather, a pair of scales with images as weights. *Jómsvikinga saga*, Chapter 20.
[2] *Hallfrethar saga*, Chapter 6.

83

Old.[3] Einar skálaglamm belongs to the third generation in the direct
male line from Bjorn the Easterner in Borgarholt and is a near kinsman
of the Kjalleklings who were bent on "dirtying" the sacrosanct
meadow on the Thórsness. There is no reason for considering Einar of a
different disposition, in matters of faith, from his kinsmen and forebears.

Here in Iceland have been found two miniature figurines dating from
the Viking Period. These finds prove that the ideas of the saga writers
about this kind of images are not pure fancy. In heathen times it was the
custom, at least in some districts, to have such figurines about one. One
of these was found in the landtake of Helgi the Lean, the son of Eyvind
the Easterner. The other turned up where the Frey worshipper Thorkel
the Tall and Geiri the Easterner, the father of the skald Glúm, first took
possession of land. With all its wealth of antiquities from the Viking
Age, Norway has no parallels to these images. Such are known, on the
other hand, from Sweden, the land of Frey worshippers. About these
Icelandic figurines Håkon Shetelig expresses himself as follows: "They
are two small human figures or images as do not have their likes in
Norway, and there is nothing similar to them except some miniature
bronze figurines from Sweden."[4]

In the fall of 1936 Shetelig visited Iceland and on this occasion
inspected our collection of antiquities. He wrote a most notable article
about his observations there. He was greatly astonished to come upon
very numerous specimens of East Scandinavian workmanship and style
from the Viking Period. In this connection he mentions "two small
circular fibulas with bronze platelets attached to them by tiny chains,"
and remarks: "Ornaments fashioned in this wise and dating from the
Viking Age have never been found in Norway, but are particularly
characteristic of Baltic style in the apparel of women." And then he
calls to mind two bronze saddle rings which to him seem to "indicate

[3] *Ibid.*, Chapter 9.
[4] "Islands graver og oldsaker fra vikingatiden," *Viking*, I (1937), 205–207. They
are now generally considered to be images of Thór. See Kristján Eldjárn, *Kuml og
Haugfé* (Reykjavík, 1956), pp. 361 f.

Swedish-Baltic influence in Iceland," and also six chapes of sword scabbards, likewise of bronze. About these chapes he has this to say among other things: "Nowhere, except in Sweden along the Baltic and in Russia, do these chapes exhibit so clearly an event in cultural life as they do in Iceland. This cannot be explained in any other way than that the Icelanders from the very beginning of their history broke away to have independent cultural intercourse and commercial relations, by-passing Norway, so that they at so early a time felt themselves not only as emigrated Norwegians but rather proceeded in their own way as a separate nation. It may seem that the chapes of scabbards are rather insignificant objects; but we shall be permitted to take them into such significant account for the reason that few antiquities from the Viking Period have been preserved in Iceland, and furthermore because we are dealing here not with imported artifacts, but rather with some early Icelandic objects of bronze fashioned after models foreign to Norway."

The accounts in our sources of the figurines are associated with two court skalds and the progenitors of prominent skald families. In all likelihood these accounts originated in those tracts of the Vatnsdale and the Hvammfjord settlements so eminently given to fertility worship and so rich in skalds. Our next task will be to consider the localities where were found the objects which the famous Norwegian archaeologist believes especially point to Swedish-Baltic influence in our country. It will be well at the same time to pay attention to other cultural memories in the vicinity of the places where these finds were made. The two figurines from the Eyjafjord and the Lake Mývatn tracts referred to above give some hope of results in advance, though the opposite might be expected before the matter is investigated. We shall begin our observations with the Eastland, continuing west from there, and then southward until we have accounted for all the finding places of these Swedish-Baltic objects and have taken into consideration the cultural attitudes prevailing in their neighborhood.

First, the fibula found in an ancient tumulus near the farmstead of

Vathi in Skrithdale. This farm lies near the coast, at the foot of the
Hallormsstathir Ridge. It is but a short distance from there to Mjóaness,
the dwelling of the skald and grove worshipper Helgi Ásbjarnarson.
The tract was first taken into possession by the brothers Ketil and
Graut-Atli, the sons of Thithrandi. In the Droplaugarsona saga[5] we are
told that they moved north of the Hallormsstathir Ridge and settled by
Lake Lagarfljót in Atlavík and at Arneitharstathir. Also, that "the
brothers constantly sailed to other lands with their wares and grew very
wealthy." From them is descended the Eastland lineage which one may
regard as the most noteworthy in the cultural history of those parts. I
venture to assert that little would be known about the ancient inhabitants of the Eastland if it had not been for them. There exist in our old
literature some twenty independent sagas and *thættir* (short stories)
which deal with persons and matters of the Eastern Quarter during the
Saga Period. Practically all of them, with the exception of Hrafnkels
saga, revolve about the descendants of Thithrandi and their relatives. It
is quite probable that none of the highborn families there in the East
achieved entrance into the saga material before intermarrying with the
descendants of Thithrandi. The family traditions of the Krossvíkings
and the people of Sítha begin when the sisters from Arneitharstathir,
Hallkatla and Jóreith, the daughters of Thithrandi, become the
mistresses in Krossvík and at Hof in the Alptafjord. The same is true
about the inception of the sagas which deal with the Hofverja clan in
the Vápnafjord. To be sure, the first of these sagas is named the saga of
Thorstein the White, the man who took possession of the land about
Hof. But one can hardly say that this saga is mainly about him, for the
kernel of the story clearly is the slaying of his brothers-in-law Einar
Thórisson, the son of Graut-Atli of Atlavík, and Thorgils Thorsteinsson
of Hof. Thorgils was married to Ásvor, the daughter of Thórir, the son
of Graut-Atli. The Vápnfirthinga saga and the *thátt* about Thorstein
stangahogg deal with their descendants. But there are no sagas about
the brothers and sisters of Thorgils or their offspring. Indeed, except for

[5] *Droplaugarsona saga*, Chapter 2.

Thorgils, the son-in-law of Thórir in Atlavík, the names of the children of Thorstein the White are known only from the family pedigree.

Now it might be thought that Thórir Thithrandi's uncommon good fortune in being blessed with good and notable offspring, or the distinction of his family, was the main reason for their occurring so often in the sagas. But how about the great clans of Thorgeir Vestarson and of Hrollaug Rognvaldsson, who also had their habitations in the Eastland? They likewise had the office of *gothi*, and no doubt various descendants of theirs were great chieftains and persons of importance in very memorable events. Yet no sagas deal with them. In general, there were no traditions worth mentioning involving the descendants of Hrollaug and Thorgeir except such where their lives and those of the descendants of Thithrandi touched. It is easy to adduce proof of this assertion. That large-hearted landtaker, Brynjólf the Old, the son of Thorgeir Vésteinsson, according to the authors of the Book of Settlements had thirteen children. Seven are mentioned by name, and the descendants of four of them are traced, with the male lineage of possessors of a *gothi*dom among them. Whenever *gothar* from this family appear in the sagas of the Eastern Quarter, they are mere supernumeraries. Yet they dwelled in the Fljótsdale District in the vicinity of the *gothar* of the kindred of Thórir Thithrandi and Hrafnkel Freysgothi, about whom there were sagas. As to the many branches descended from Brynjólf the Old, the sagas deal only with the progeny of Ásvor, his daughter, who was the wife of Thórir, the son of Graut-Atli.

It is unnecessary to discuss this matter at greater length. We have it in writing that the old sagas about the Eastfirthings concern themselves mainly with the descendants of the brothers Ketil thrym and Graut-Atli. As to the Hrafnkels saga, we can say that it contains little of old traditions, as Sigurthur Nordal has shown convincingly.[6] Thus the kin of Thithrandi certainly occupy a particular position in the cultural history of the Eastern Quarter, and this particular position is manifested in the preservation of tradition in that kin. There is only one explana-

[6] *Hrafnkatla* (*Studia Islandica* No. 7, 1940), p. 41.

tion for this: The descendants of Thithrandi from the very beginning laid more weight on preserving the memory of their forebears than any other family in the Eastland. We possess information of one descendant of Thithrandi who retold the saga of kinsmen who had passed away long before his time. That was Thorvald Ingjaldsson, the great grandson of the skald Grím Droplaugarson of Arneitharstathir.[7] I suspect that one of this family was the skald and purveyor of legendary lore Arnald Thorvaldsson, who is responsible for a substantial share of Saxo Grammaticus' History of the Danes.[8] There is presumptive evidence for that. But let us not discuss that for the time being. However that be, we do know as a fact that the kin of Thithrandi were from of old most partial to handing down traditional lore. With them, the fixation of tradition was a family characteristic.

The main branch of the Thithrandi kin grew up in the inland region of Lake Lagarfljót, the tract, that is, where the "Swedish-Baltic" ornamental fibula was found. There likewise in heathen times dwelled the descendants of Hrafnkel Freysgothi; and there, at some place in the neighborhood of Vath, was the temple of Steinvor the Priestess. Here also are found two of the three place names in the Eastland in which Frey is the first element. The third is in the Oræfa District where, as we know, the Freysgythlings, the kinsmen of Bjorn the Easterner, maintained sacrifices to Frey. In that family, as we know, priestesses had charge of the sacrifices, because Thuríth, the sister of Thórth Freysgothi, is called the temple priestess. By Lake Lagarfljót in saga times there dwelled those skalds, in the Múlathing District, of whom we have verses. Nowhere else, in the entire East- and Southland, have accounts of sacrifices to Frey been preserved, except in the localities where the families of these skalds resided. We learn that such sacrifices were performed at Oddsstathir in the Skógar District. In this same small tract

---

[7] *Droplaugarsona saga*, Chapter 15.

[8] Saxo Grammaticus, Danish historian and poet (*ca.* 1150–1206). In his *Gesta Danorum*, *sub anno* 1167, Arnald is mentioned as one of Archbishop Absalon's followers.

there were hills named after Frey. Both these farms stood north below the Hallormsstathir Ridge, and south of it lies Vath, where the fibula turned up. It is of importance to note this.

Now, as to the fibula from Gautland in the Lake Mývatn District: The account of the sacrifice to Frey at Oddsstathir, the home of Odd sindri, has the same appearance as that of the one performed by Thorkel the Tall, who took land south of Lake Mývatn and lived at Grœnavatn. The old sagas do not mention any other Frey worshipper in the region between the Oræfa District and the Eyjafjord except these two and also Hrafnkel Freysgothi. The farm Baldrsheim in the Lake Mývatn tract doubtless was established on the landtake of Thorkel the Tall. There, in a tumulus, was found one of the figurines. So the neighborhood of Geiri the Easterner and Thorkel the Tall yielded two of the twelve antiquities which Shetelig avers bear testimony to East Scandinavian cultural influences in our country.

As to the chapes found at Lund in Fnjóskadale: This farm was established by the grove worshipper and skald Thórir snepil, the son of a daughter of the lawman Thórgný in Sweden. East of the Eyjafjord and in the South no settlers are accounted to be of East Scandinavian origin except Thórir snepil and Uni the Dane. Now it is also to be borne in mind that there are three skalds from the Thingeyrasveit District whose verse has come down to us, viz., Thórir snepil of Lund farm, Hallstein of Hofthi, and Glúm Geirason of Geirastathir by Lake Mývatn. The antiquities above referred to were found remarkably close to their homesteads. The descendants of Thórir snepil, viz., Helgi the Lean and Gnúpa-Bárth play a role in the sagas from the Thingeyjar and the Eyjafjord Districts. Thus these families are analogous to the descendants of Hrafnkel and of Thithrandi in the Fljótsdale District. The kin of Ingimund the Old in Vatnsdale are of the same nature. No one is likely to doubt that much handing down of tradition took place in that family. In all the old North Quarter east of Vatnsdale there is hardly a trace of Frey worship, except in the case of Thorkel the Tall and the descendants of Helgi the Lean. At Hripkelsstathir there existed

a temple dedicated to Frey, and at Thverá there was a great Frey
sanctuary. In the same parish, at Eyrarland, the Eyjafjord miniature was
found. That farm was established on the land along Fiskilæk Creek
belonging to Thorgeir. Thorgeir was the son-in-law of Helgi the Lean.
It may now be clearly discerned of how great an importance the finding
places of the miniatures are, when at the same time we consider the
traditions of the Vatnsdalers about the figurine belonging to Ingimund
and the one of Hallfreth vandræthaskald. In the Vatnsdale there existed
a temple dedicated to Frey in which a priestess officiated. There, too,
originated the tradition about the horse Freyfaxi which was owned by
Faxa-Brand and which so definitely reminds us of the story of Freyfaxi
handed down by the family of Hrafnkel in the Fljótsdale area. We called
attention above to the fact that it was not by accident that stories about
swine were associated with the names of Ingimund the Old, Hrafnkel
Freysgothi, and Helgi the Lean; and now it becomes even clearer than
before that it is no mere coincidence that it is precisely Ingimund, Helgi,
and Thórir snepil who are forced to seek shelter inland from the cold
north winds. The traditions of Frey worship in the Vatnsdale and
around the Eyjafjord, concerning the grove worship of Thórir snepil,
together with the "Swedish-Baltic" antiquities demonstrate that with
sufficient clearness, even though other evidence be lacking. The families
of Helgi, Thórir, and Ingimund are of East Scandinavian origin; all
show the same distinctive cultural characteristics, viz., the retention of
traditions, skaldship, Frey veneration.

As to the chape found near Tannstatha Bank on the eastern shore of
the Hrútafjord: Bálki Blæingsson from Sótaness was the first to take
possession of lands about the Hrútafjord. Sótaness is one of the coastal
settlements of West Gautland, in the province of Ranríki. This is now a
part of Sweden, but in olden times was a bone of contention between
the kings of Norway and those of Sweden. Bersi the Godless, the son of
Bjálki, lived very close to the Tannstatha Bank before he removed himself south to Langavatnsdale. One of his grandsons was the skald Bjorn
Hitdælakappi, about whom there is a long saga. To the same family

belongs the skald Holmgongu-Bersi, who plays a considerable role in the Kormáks saga. Ogmund of Mel farm, Kormák's father, is reported to be of Vík (Norway) origin. He settled in the landtake of Bjorn, the father of Mithfjarthar-Skeggi. Bjorn was called Skinna-Bjorn (Pelt-B.) "because he was a trader to Holmgarth" (Russia).[9] From the dwelling places of the people living about the Mithfjord which we have just mentioned, it is but a very short distance to Tannstatha Bank. Close by it is found the fourth place name, and the only one preserved in our land beside those of the East Quarter, which shows the compositional element Frey, viz., Freysbakki (F.'s Bank). The farm so named was situated on Vatnsness at the mouth of the Mithfjord. Old deeds make it clear that the church at Mel owned the foreshore and what drifted onto it. This calls to mind the appellation Freysnesfjara (F.-foreshore) in the Oræfa District and suggests that sometimes strands where trees or whales are found drifted ashore may have been dedicated to Frey. The Kormáks saga tells us that the sons of Dalla at Mel had first call to the whales driven ashore on Vatnsness, and this statement probably owes its origin to old rights of the people at Mel to the Freysivík Banks. It is thought that the temple of the Mithfjord people stood on land belonging to Mel, right close to the Steinstathir farm of Thorveig, the witch whom the skald Kormák is said to have driven away.[10] Thus one may suppose that to Frey belonged both the flotsam and jetsam and the temple in the Freysivík, and that when a church was erected at Mel to take the place of the temple, it inherited the right to what had drifted on the strand of Vatnsness. The sorceress Thorveig is likely to have been the temple priestess of the people about the Mithfjord, just as Steinvor, the kinswoman of Brodd-Helgi, was the temple priestess of the people of Fljótsdale, Thuríth, the daughter of Solmund, the temple priestess of the Vatnsdalers, and Frithgerth, the daughter of Thórth in Hvamm, the temple priestess of the Dalesmen about the Hvammsfjord. When Kormák drove old Thorveig from Steinstathir, she sought help from

[9] *Ldn.* § 221.
[10] *Kormáks saga*, Chapter 5.

Holmgongu-Bersi, which would indicate that she belonged to his kin. "Bersi bought land for her north of the Hrútafjord, and she lived there for a long time."[11] It is obvious from the account in the saga that its author considered the new dwelling place of Thorveig to be about where the farm Tannstatha Banks now stands. Round about Thorveig's dwelling, on both sides of the Hrútafjord, there thrived in the olden times such a multitude of skalds that no parallel example is found elsewhere on so small and sparsely populated a tract as are the regions about the Mithfjord and the Hrútafjord.

Now, as to the saddle ring found near Hálsar in the Vatnsfjord. It was here that Snæbjorn, the son of Eyvind the Easterner took land. Another of the chapes was found somewhere in the Ísafjarthardjúp region. The exact location is not known, but it was sent to the National Collection of Antiquities from the Ísafjord trading post. In all likelihood the finding place was the Skutulsfjord or its vicinity, where Helgi Hrólfsson, the son of Helgi the Lean, a kinsman of Snæbjorn of Vatnsfjord, took land. Still another chape, showing the same workmanship, was found at Kirkjubólsdale in the Dýrafjord, a short distance from Hof. The finding place probably is in the landtake of Véstein Végeirsson. Véstein "took land between Hálsar (Ridges) in the Dýrafjord and lived in Haukadale."[12] From this statement in the Book of Settlements we may infer that Véstein's landtake embraced more territory than only Haukadale, and the Kirkjubóls Dale is the next settlement to the south. To the north his lands were bounded by the landtake of one Eirík, who took possession of Keldudale and lived there. In the passage of the Gísla saga Súrssonar dealing with genealogy,[13] in the Book of Settlements Véstein Végeirsson is characterized by the sobriquet "Easterner," like Geiri, the father of the skald Glúm in the Reykdæla saga, and Eyvind, the father of Helgi the Lean and Snæbjorn. And now there appears an astonishing circumstance: The settlers who in the Book of Settlements

11 *Ibid.*, Chapter 7.
12 *Ldn.* § 187.
13 *Gísla saga Súrssonar*, Chapter 4.

and the sagas of the Icelanders bear the surname of Easterlings or Easterners, or in some other way are characterized as of East Scandinavian origin, are scarcely more numerous than the Swedish-Baltic antiquities Shetelig mentions.

We have discussed the nine places where these antiquities were found. It seems that all these objects were located in the landtake, or in the neighborhood of, men from East Scandinavia, and right close to their dwelling places. This is the case with the chapes from Kirkjubóls Dale, Tannstathir Bank, and Lund, the two antiquities from Lake Mývatn, the image from Eyrarland, and the saddle ring from Hálshús. The chape from the Ísafjord and the fibula from Vath may be put with these for the time being. These seven antiquities demonstrate clearly that we cannot speak of chance. It should be added that the reports about the figurines are associated with the great grandson of Bjorn the Easterner, with Ingimund the Old, who is of Gautish origin on his mother's side, and with Hallfreth vandræthaskáld, who moved to Gautland.

Scholars will probably agree that Frey worship was brought to Norway from Sweden. Memories of that are found more especially in northern Norway. Magnus Olsen[14] thinks that this religious tendency first took root there in the last centuries of heathendom, even before the beginning of the Viking Age. We have observed that traces of Frey worship in Iceland are associated with the landtake, and in the neighborhood, of persons of East Scandinavian origin and around the finding places of Swedish-Baltic antiquities. In the neighborhood of Vath there are two place names containing Frey as an element, a temple priestess, and memories of sacrifices to Frey. In the tract about Lake Mývatn there lived a Frey worshipper, at Lund, a grove worshipper; in the Eyjafjord region we find a temple dedicated to Frey, traditions of sacrifice to him, and seasons sacred to him; in Vatnsdale there are a Frey temple, a temple priestess, and traditions of Frey, and, finally, in the Mithfjord, in the precinct adjoining the Hrútafjord, place names showing Frey. From the Westfjord Quarter we have only one account

[14] *Farms and Fanes of Ancient Norway* (Oslo, 1928), Chapter 9.

of sacrifices performed to Frey, that is, in Haukadale, the landtake of Véstein the Easterner. From there, as observed above, it is but a short distance to Kirkjubóls Dale. Let be the fact that no accounts of sacrifices to Frey have come down to us from the Ísafjartherdjúp region. Yet that very probably represents the belief of the settlers there, viz., of Helgi Hrólfsson and Snæbjorn in the Vatnsfjord, especially when regard is had to their near kinsfolk in the Eyjafjord District.

In the section entitled "Skalds, Swine, Saur- Farms" I adduced arguments in proof that Freysgothi Thorgrím Thorsteinsson took up the fertility worship, following the example of his maternal kinsfolk, the people of Hvamm in the Dales District. With him are associated the Haukadale traditions of Frey. Thorgrím was buried in a mound at Sæból in the Haukadale; and the Gísla saga Súrssonar[15] has this to say about this mound, that "snow never lay on the south side of Thorgrím's burial mound, nor did it ever freeze there, and men surmised that he was so dear to Frey, on account of his sacrifices to him, that the god would not wish any frost to come between them." Thorgrím had been brought up at Helgafell "and became the temple priest as soon as he was old enough for that," as says the author of the Eyrbyggja saga.[16] As a young man he moved west to Haukadale and became the chieftain of the people around the Dýrafjord on its west side. Their temple was located in Kirkjubóls Dale, and that is where the chape was found. There is little doubt that a temple to Frey was located there. The same holds regarding the temple at Hofstathir in the Helgafell District when the Thór worshipper Thorstein Thorskabít passed away, and the one at Hvamm in the Dales District. Thóra, the mother of Thorgrím Freysgothi hailed from Hvamm. Ólaf feilan, her father, was the son of a daughter of Eyvind the Easterner and the grandson of Auth the Deepminded, the sister of Bjorn the Easterner. Ari fróthi traces the genealogy of the Hvamm kin to the Yngling kings, who are said to be descended from Frey. We are told that when Thorvald the Wide-farer

---

[15] *Gísla saga*, Chapter 18.
[16] *Eyrbyggja saga*, Chapter 12.

preached Christianity in Hvamm,[17] Frithgerth, Thórth's daughter, who was the mistress there, performed a sacrifice in the temple at the very time he preached Christianity. In the stanza of Thorvald about this occurrence Frithgerth is called a priestess. Round about the Hvamms-fjord there lived on every farm the descendants of Auth the Deep-minded and her brother, Bjorn the Easterner, their relations, and their wards. Judging from the experience gathered concerning the finding places of Swedish-Baltic antiquities as discussed above, one would expect to find such objects, if anywhere in Iceland, then right here. We know that here East Scandinavian Frey worshippers had in their hands the administration of the laws—men whom we may unhesitatingly count among the strongest promoters of Old Icelandic skaldship and the preservation of tradition. And precisely there came to light two antiquities of Swedish-Baltic workmanship: a chape, discovered in the Ljárskóg region, and a saddle ring, found between the farms Glerárskóg and Ljárskóg. Thus both these objects derive from the innermost section of the landtake of Auth the Deep-minded, that tract which she left to Ólaf feilan, her grandson. At the same time, we should call to mind that Snæbjorn from the Vatnsfjord, who took land where the saddle ring of East Scandinavian workmanship turned up, was the maternal uncle of Ólaf feilan.

The twelfth, and last, antiquity is a chape which was found in an ancient mound close by the farmhouse of Hafr-Bjarnarstathir on Rosm-whaleness. In it a chieftain was interred, together with his weapons, among them an unusually beautiful sword with the chape. The farm name indicates positively that originally there lived here one Hafr-Bjorn, a son of Molda-Gnúp Hrólfsson, a landtaker from Moldatún in North Mœr (Norway). According to the Book of Settlements, the sons of Molda-Gnúp took possession of Grindavík, and from there it is not far to Hafr-Bjarnarstathir. But the most important thing in this matter is that the name Hafr-Bjorn is exceptional in Old Icelandic history and probably occurs nowhere except in this family. Here, then,

[17] *Kristni saga,* Chapter 2.

we may with great probability assign this thousand-year-old ornamental antiquity to a definite family. Here, finally, there has come to light an object of Swedish-Baltic workmanship not from a saga district. However, skaldic culture evidently did thrive in the Molda-Gnúp family. The Book of Settlements quotes stanzas by Vémund, the paternal uncle of Hafr-Bjorn; and the daughters of his brother, Geirný at Mosfell and Rannveig at Hjalli, both had sons who became court skalds. Though no separate saga deals particularly with Molda-Gnúp and his progeny, one may conclude from the account given of him in the Book of Settlements that the preservation of tradition ran strongly in his family. It may very well be that the scarcity of people and the few farms on Reykjaness in the olden times had much to do with there not being a district or a family saga.

Now the circular journey from Vath in Skrithdale west and south around our land is completed, and that journey has borne surprising results. It has made it evident that the preservation of traditions, skaldship, and Swedish-Baltic taste in the fashioning, or else the choice, of ornamental objects must have been interwoven strands in the culture of individual families and districts in heathen times. I shall willingly admit that it may seem improbable that such distantly related lines of culture as are involved here were closely associated. But there is no escaping the facts. Let us make the same circular journey in reverse, and then we shall see even more clearly how the matter shapes up. First we come to Ljárskóg, the homestead of Thorstein Kuggason. As Sigurthur Nordal has pointed out,[18] there probably existed a separate saga about him. Everywhere about Ljárskóg there lived the main personages of the Laxdæla saga. Here also played the lost sagas of Thórth gellir and Thorgils Holluson; and the Eyrbyggja saga and Víga-Glúms saga deal with the kinsmen of the people of Hvamm in the Helgafell vicinity. There is no need to dwell at length on the skaldship of this neighborhood. The saga about the skald Gísli Súrsson has the Dýrafjord region,

[18] *Literaturhistorie, B Norge og Island, Nordisk Kultur*, Vol. VIII (Oslo, 1953), 247.

along with the Haukadale, as the scene of its main action. In it the sons of Véstein the Easterner, Auth and Véstein, have leading roles. It is important to mention them particularly, because in the Book of Settlements we are informed that there was "a long saga" about Vébjorn Sygnakappi, their paternal uncle. He took land west in the Ísafjarthardjúp region in the neighborhood of the two kinsmen Snæbjorn in the Vatnsfjord and Helgi Hrólfsson. Both the Hávarthar saga and the Fóstbrœthra saga are located in this district, where in saga times there lived also four skalds mentioned by name, viz., Volu-Stein, Thormóth Kolbrúnarskáld, Hávarth the Halt, and Ólaf bjarnylr. So the regions west about the Ísafjarthardjúp counted among those in our country prominent with skalds, even though their number bears no comparison with the tracts around Tannstathir Bank and the settlements about the Hrútafjord and the Mithfjord. From these districts we have the Kormáks saga, the Grettis saga, the Bandamanna saga, and also the *thættir* dealing with Odd Ófeigsson and the skalds Hrómund the Halt of Fagrabrekka and Hrafn from the Hrútafjord.

When we leave Vatnsdale with its sagas about the families of Ingimund and of Hallfreth vandræthaskáld which preserved memories of the figurines owned by their ancestors, our path leads through districts which lack both traditions and skalds, until we come to the Eyrar land and the Eyjafjord. Then there opens before us a veritable skald district. Out by the shore of the fjord lived Hallstein Thengilsson, and inland, Víga-Glúm, his son Vigfús, Eyjólf Valgertharson and his son Einar, Eilíf Guthrúnarson and his wife, Thordís skáldkona, also Brúsi Hallason. This is the scene of the Víga-Glúms saga, which deals also with the Eyfirthing kin, the descendants of Helgi the Lean, who all play a more or less important role in the Ljósvetninga saga, the Reykdæla saga, and the Valla-Ljóts saga. The neighborhood of the Eyjafjord is the scene of the lost Esphælinga saga. It is said to have dealt much with Thórth Hrafnsson of Stokkahlathir. He was of the third generation in the direct male line from Thórir snepil at Lund. About Thórarin, the son of Thórth, there exists a separate *thátt* which goes with the Ljósvetninga saga. One may say that both this saga and the Reykdæla saga begin with accounts of the sons-in-law of Thorkel the Black. He was the grandfather of Thórth of Stokkahlathir and the son of Thórir snepil. This branch, like the Mýrar kin, had its origin on Hrafnista Island (Norway). An unusually large amount of tradition lived in that family, and it is safe to designate the descendants of Thórir snepil and Helgi the Lean as those families which preserved the greatest amount of traditional lore in the Northland east of Vatnsdale. There exists a great amount of tradition about the landtakers Thorkel the Tall and Geiri the Easterner who settled about Lake Mývatn; likewise a great many traditions about their descendants have come down to us. The Reykdæla saga, the Víga-Glúms saga, and the Laxdæla saga bear witness to that.

Now we approach again the end of our journey. We abandon the saga districts about Thingeyrar and the Eyjafjord with their many East Scandinavian antiquities, and proceed to the Fljótsdale District. Once more we are in a saga region which it is very worth while considering. Here originated the Droplaugarsona saga, the Brandkrossa *thátt*, the Hrafnkels saga, and the saga of Gunnar Thithrandabani. In this region the kin of Thithrandi have, more than other families, put their stamp on cultural life from the earliest colonization. The example of his descendants and how they dominated the history of the Eastfjords District throws a sharp light on one of the most important aspects of Old Icelandic culture. A number of chieftainly families here laid particular stress on the composition of verse and the preservation of traditions. Naturally, the memories of their own forebears were given chief consideration. From the choice of these traditions in our old literature we can draw conclusions about the nature of these families, and it is these families that play the chief role in the world of the saga. That is not saying, of course, that they were concerned with more important and more memorable events than had happened in many other families, memories which now are for the most part or altogether forgotten.

It will hardly be called open to question that East Scandinavian taste and style, especially in heathen times, prevailed in the sections most notable for traditions and skalds. I shall not discuss here whether these Swedish-Baltic antiquities were produced at home or imported. That is of no importance in this connection. The gist of the matter is that East Scandinavian taste in the arts happens to be one of the main characteristics of the great skald families. I have demonstrated before that skaldic culture was brought to our land with fertility worshippers. Now, still further, it has become unmistakably evident that memories, in traditions and names, relating to sacrifices to Frey nearly without exception, are associated with proximity to the finding places of East Scandinavian antiquities. Possibly most important of all, though, is the fact that most of these antiquities are found in the neighborhood of the dwelling places of those colonists who in plain words are called, or are considered to be, of East Scandinavian origin. All this proves that the springs of Icelandic skaldship are to be sought in the lands east of Norway. To the same source are to be ascribed what are believed to be the memories of the oldest poetry in the Northlands. Again, the composition, among East Scandinavians, of epic poetry must be ascribed to the period of the Migration of Nations. But in Norway this poetic culture appears not to have taken root before the very latest times of heathendom, at the same time as the East Scandinavian worship of Frey. Now it becomes even clearer why in Iceland skaldship flourished most in the proximity of temples dedicated to Frey and in the tracts with *saur-* farms and such as have women's names as their first element. The most prominent members in the Northlands of that branch of the race which laid most stress on poetry dwelled but a short time in Norway before sailing west, some of them stopping but a brief time on the coast lands of Norway. It is the last-named families who transported to Iceland the Viking Period's Swedish-Baltic taste in the arts. The account of the short-lived stay of Bjorn, the father of Eyvind the Easterner, in the Hvinisfjord (Norway) is significant. Bjorn must have come to Norway from east in Sweden. He chooses a dwelling place for himself in the Hvinisfjord in the Agthir District, and from there he goes in summer on viking expeditions to the west. "Later on Eyvind came from the east to join his father Bjorn," and "took over the warships of his father and the latter's occupation when he became weary of warfare."[19] Soon Eyvind settles down permanently in the Hebrides or in Ireland. There he begets two sons who take possession of land in Iceland. A thousand years later there are found, on the landtake of both, antiquities of East Scandinavian origin and, furthermore, two such objects on the landtake of Bjorn's nephew. Thus the use of Swedish-Baltic ornamental objects evidently was of great importance in the habitations of the late-comers among the East Scandinavian families. In those localities the ground very likely to this very day conceals a considerable number of that kind of antiquities.

If one may make an inference from the account of the Book of Settlements about the outfitting of warships by Bjorn and his son, Eyvind the Easterner, in the Hvinisfjord, we must suppose that about the middle of the ninth century there was in that place a colony of East Scandinavian vikings. It was in Hvinir, in the close neighborhood of the *hersir* Grím Kolbjarnarson, that Bjorn settled when he came to Norway. Grím is said to have been akin to the *hersir* Arinbjorn, whose wife was the daughter of the skald Bragi Boddason the Old. From them the Gilsbekkings are descended. Bragi is said to have been the skald of two kings of Sweden. Thjóthólf the Wise (or Learned) composed the poem Ynglingatal (Enumeration of the Ynglings) about the ancient Uppsala kings. He lived in Hvinir, as did the kinsmen of the *hersir* Arinbjorn. Thjóthólf leaned on old East Scandinavian traditions and, of course, also on ancient lays, brought to Agthir by East Scandinavians. It is thought that the chief residence of the viking hosts who about the middle of the ninth century harried in Scotland and Ireland was in the Norwegian districts of Vík, Agthir, and Rogaland. The foremost of the viking kings in Norway at that time was Guthröth Rognvaldsson, the father of Ólaf, king of Dublin. According to Irish

[19] *Ldn.* § 264.

annal fragments[20] from that time King Guthröth must have levied taxes on the Irish. But about 870 there was a rebellion against him in Norway. Gustav Storm[21] considers Guthröth and Ólaf to have been the leaders of the host which gave battle to King Harald in the Hafrsfjord. In that battle various men took part who later sailed to Iceland, thus Bálki of Sótaness, Ingimund the Old, and Thránd the Much Sailing from Hvinir, the brother of Eyvind the Easterner.

The author of *Ágrip af Noregskonunga sǫgum* (Summary of the Sagas about the Kings of Norway) seems to have known traditions of the battle in the Hafrsfjord which do not appear elsewhere in the ancient literature. In this matter he apparently leans on lays, and has the king who commanded the fleet opposed to King Harald flee to Denmark and fall, later on, in a battle on Wendish soil.[22] Historians do not seem to have taken cognizance of this tradition. But when we consider the presence of East Scandinavian antiquities in Iceland and the words of Thorbjorn hornklofi about the *austkylfur* (see above, page 68) in the Battle of the Hafrsfjord and about the Eastern maidens in the possession of the victors, this tradition about the flight and fall of the king (Guthröth) is worth our serious attention. The chief colony of East Scandinavian vikings in the Baltic was called Kylfingaland. And the finds of antiquities in the lands bordering the East Baltic make it evident that East Scandinavian vikings and merchants were domiciled there for a long time before the viking expeditions to Ireland and Scotland began, starting from their Norwegian base. Hence there is no contradiction in an East Scandinavian people's having had at the same time a residence there and domination west of the North Sea as well as in lands north and east of the Baltic. Thus it may very well be that it was King Guthröth Rognvaldsson who sought refuge in Denmark after his defeat in the Hafrsfjord and later fell east in Wendland. There will be opportunity later to go into this matter when we discuss the Ynglings.

[20] *Annals of Ireland: Three Fragments*, ed. John O'Donovan (Dublin, 1860).
[21] *Norsk Historisk Tidsskrift*, anden række, II (1880), 321 f.
[22] *Ágrip*, Chapter 2.

Håkon Shetelig claimed[23] that "the Icelanders, from the very beginning of their history, cleared their way to independent cultural intercourse and commercial connections, bypassing Norway, so that even
in the earliest times they were not only Norwegians who had emigrated, but rather proceeded on their own way as a separate nation."
This bold conclusion is based on the East Scandinavian antiquities
which have been unearthed here. I agree with it so far as to consider the
Icelanders of the tenth century a distinct people, but it is altogether
preposterous to regard the men who brought East Scandinavian culture
to Iceland as "emigrated Norwegians." The conjecture that the Icelanders cleared their way to an independent cultural intercourse with
East Scandinavian lands evidently springs from Shetelig's unshakable
belief in their Norwegian origin. There was no possibility of explaining
the great difference between Icelandic and Norwegian antiquities by
alleging it to have resulted through Celtic influence. So there was no
other way out of his difficulties than the one he chose, and he did not
hesitate. "It is easy to explain these Swedish influences on Iceland by
assuming journeys about the Baltic. It is but natural that the artistic
taste of the people in Iceland took another direction than to Norway,"
says Shetelig. However, one may ask: How is it that Norwegian
merchants and vikings who sailed the Baltic did not succumb to the
same cultural influences as Icelanders? Was the Baltic perchance closed
to the Norwegians but open to Icelandic sailors? And should there not
have been considerable cultural intercourse and dealings between
Norway and Sweden in the Viking Age? These questions, though they
are not answered, suffice to show of how little cogency Shetelig's
conclusions are. At the same time, he is right in believing that the
explanation of the Icelanders' taste in their choice of ornamental objects
lies at hand. Like their preservation of traditions, their skaldic culture,
and their Frey worship, it is an inheritance from their East Scandinavian
forebears.

[23] "Islands graver og oldsaker fra vikingatiden," 201.

# 5. Skalds, Names, Genealogies

"Gaut dwelled in Gautsdale. He was one-armed. He and Eyvind sorkvir committed suicide, not wanting to live after Ingimund the Old."[1] Geirmund heljarskin "married Herríth, the daughter of Gaut Gautreksson the Open-handed."[2] In the verse which Thórir snepil composed about his departure from Kaldakin he has this to say: "But we, Hjálmun-Gaut and I, departed safely."[3] According to the authors of the Book of Settlements, the fathers of the landtakers Geirmund, Ingimund, and Thórir all married East Scandinavian women. Note the number three. And the three sons also are in agreement in being joined in close relationship with men who bore the name of Gaut. With that all persons in the Book of Settlements bearing that name have been mentioned. Very evidently we have here before us a remarkable subject for investigation.

From saga times two men occur who are named Gaut, viz., farmer Gaut of Gautlands and Gaut Sleituson, "a kinsman" of Thórarin ofsi of Stokkahlathir in the Eyjafjord region. Thórarin probably is kin to Thórir snepil. In addition, I have come upon seven Icelandic place names showing the element Gaut, and they all appear to be from ancient times. They are as follows: Gautlands in the Lake Mývatn parish, Gautsstathir on Svalbarth Strand, Gautsdale and Gautsgil (G. ravine) in the Bolstatharhlíth parish, Gautshamar (G. crag) in the Steingrímsfjord region, Gautsdale in the Króksfjord, and finally Gautsstathagróf (G. pit) in the Helgafell parish. Gautlands farm is in the proximity of Geirastathir. There at first lived Geir the Easterner, the father of the skald Glúm. Father and son removed themselves to the Króksfjord and

[1] *Ldn.* § 231.     [2] *Ldn.* § 162.     [3] *Ldn.* § 284.

103

dwelt there at Geirastathir. Brynjólfur of Minna-Núp has pointed out[4] that this farm now probably is called Ingunnarstathir, after Ingunn, the wife of the skald Glúm. Gautsdale in the Króksfjord is in the neighborhood of Ingunnarstathir. One can hardly escape the conclusion that both farms, Gautlands and Gautsdale, are called so after followers or clients of the Easterner who moved from the Lake Mývatn District to the Króksfjord. This view finds ready and strong support if we remember from where the Gaut place names came to this region. The farm of Gautsstathir on Svalbarth Strand is in the landtake of Helgi the Lean, the son of Eyvind the Easterner from Sweden. Gautsstathagróf is in the locality where Bjorn the Easterner settled; and Gautsdale and Gautsgil one may regard as names of the native place of Gaut, the friend of Ingimund the Old. The connection between the three landtakers and the (three) men called Gaut will scarcely seem mysterious as soon as we look into the matter.

Now we recollect that above were discussed three accounts dealing with figurines. They were associated with Einar skálaglamm, the descendant on the sword side of Bjorn the Easterner, and the Vatnsdale clan, with Hallfreth vandræthaskáld and Ingimund the Old, the intimate friend of Gaut of Gautsdale. There would be no need to recapitulate this were it not for the fact that the two ancient figurines found in the Vatnsdale had not come to light a short distance from Gautsstathir and Gautlands. At the same time it should be borne in mind that there are only seven place names containing the element "Gaut," three accounts about figurines, and two finds of such. One may say that this group of facts showing such distinctive traits do agree with one another in a most remarkable way. Some would perhaps remark that this is a case of coincidence. But let them take into account that one of the six East Scandinavian chapes was found in the home district of Thórir snepil, the companion of Hjálmun-Gaut, and one of the East Scandinavian fibulas, in Gautlands.

As might be expected, the names Gaut and Gauti are often found

---

[4] In *Árbók hins íslenzkra fornleifafélags* (1899), p. 7.

associated. Thórarin ofsi, the kinsman of Gaut Sleituson, is said to be the son of a daughter of one Gauti Armóthsson. In the Bolstatharhlíth parish, a short distance from Gautsdale and Gautsgil, we find the place name Gautavirki (Gauti's stronghold). Gautastathir (Gauti's stead) is the name of a farm in Horthadale. In this tract there lived in early times some of the followers of Auth the Deep-minded, the sister of Bjorn the Easterner. In the Steingrímsfjord region there are found, besides Gautshamar, the place names Gautadale (Gauti's dale) and Gautastathir. Still further, there is a Gautastathir in the Jokulsfjord region. These comprise the Gaut place names in the Westfjord Quarter, and it will be instructive, with them in mind, to reflect on the account of the landtake of Geirmund heljarskin, the son-in-law of Gaut Gautreksson: "Geirmund sailed west along the Strands and took land from Rytagnúp west to the Horn, and from there eastward to Straumsness. There he established four farms."—"Some say that he also owned a farm in Selárdale at Geirmundarstathir in the Steingrímsfjord."[5]—"Orlyg, the son of Bothvar Vígsterksson, passed the first winter with Geirmund heljarskin. But in spring Geirmund gave him a habitation in Athalvík, together with the lands adjacent."—"Orlyg took possession of Slétta and the Jokulsfjord."[6] All the Westfjord place names with Gaut are found, just as one might expect, in the parts which Geirmund's clients had chosen for their habitations. Among the settlers in the Westfjord Quarter, Geirmund is the only one to be associated in tradition with men who bore the name of Gaut or Gauti.

We have not yet mentioned among Gaut place names the Gautavík (G. bight) in the eastern Berufjord region and the farm Gautastathir in the Knappastathir parish. In this small parish there is the farm Thorgautsstathir. There, Thórth knapp took land. In the Hauksbók version of the Book of Settlements he is called "a Swede." Thorgautsstathir is the name also of a farm in Hvitarsítha, and two Asgautsstathir are found in the Southland. Five persons with the name Thorgaut, and two called Ásgaut, occur in the history of Iceland in the period of colonization and

<hr>

[5] *Ldn.* § 164.    [6] *Ldn.* § 203.

in the sagas. Thorgaut is mentioned in the Reykdæla saga. He appears
on the scene in the neighborhood of Thórir snepil and Hjálmun-Gaut,
and ends his days in the neighborhood of Gaut of the Gautlands farm.
Another Thorgaut is mentioned in the Grettis saga, where he is called a
foreigner. The account of him is connected with the family seat of
Ingimund the Old in the Vatnsdale. The third Thorgaut is from Mýrar
in the Dýrafjord. He is descended from Eyvind the Easterner. The
fourth of this name was a sailor with the settler Hrosskel, the progenitor
of the Gilsbekkings. Hrosskel is called a descendant of Erp lútandi and
Bragi the Old, both court skalds of King Bjorn of Sweden. After
Thorgaut, the sailor with Hrosskel, is named the farm Thorgautsstathir
in Hvítársítha. There, a fifth Thorgaut lived about the close of the
tenth century. Ásgaut was the name of a thrall at Goddastathir in the
Laxárdale. He fled the country and settled in Denmark. Another
Ásgaut was the son-in-law of the settler Thorkel bjálfi, a foster brother
of Ráthorm in Vetleifsholt. They both took land in Holtar, as did
Askel hnoskan, the paternal grandfather of this Ásgaut. All these
settlers arrived from west of the North Sea.

These examples make it plain as day that there is a cultural connection
in our land between East Scandinavian antiquities and the Gaut names.
One may best obtain a clearer insight into this curious relation by
observing how these antiquities and names are distributed over the four
old Quarters. Altogether there are seventeen place names showing the
compositional element "Gaut," and twelve antiquities. These are
distributed as follows:

Westfjord Quarter..... seven place names, five antiquities
North Quarter ........ seven place names, five antiquities
East Quarter .......... one place name, one antiquity
South Quarter........ two place names, one antiquity

The origin of the Norse Gaut names has been most thoroughly
studied by Elias Wessén.[7] He concludes that they originated in Sweden

[7] *De nordiska folkstammarna i Bēowulf* (Stockholm, 1927), Chapter 4. Also in
*Studier i Sveriges hedna mytologi och fornhistoria* (Uppsala Universitets Årsskrift,
1924), 81–119.

and had scarcely reached any notable spread in the Viking Period or even later. Once this is realized, one need not be surprised that East Scandinavian antiquities and the Gaut names arrived together in Iceland in the wake of those families which best preserved traditions about their East Scandinavian origin. The Eyfirthing clan best of them all kept alive memories of its East Scandinavian descent. Also, this branch appears to have come to Norway first in the middle of the ninth century. We are told in so many words that Eyvind the Easterner had come from Sweden and for this reason bore this surname. Geiri the Easterner, Véstein the Easterner, and Bjorn austræni (the Easterling) no doubt bore their sobriquet by the same right. Bjorn the Easterling is the grandson of Bjorn buna, the son-in-law of Víking, named after Scania and called Skáneyjarskelfir (Terrifier of Scania); and Eyvind the Easterner is the paternal grandson of Hrólf from Ám in Sweden. By clear illustration one may show that both families sprang from the same roots. Two Helgi Hrólfssons are mentioned in the Book of Settlements. One lived in the Skutulsfjord, the other at Hofgarthir on Snæfellsness. Their descent is as follows: Hrólf from Ám—Bjorn—Eyvind the Easterner— Helgi the Lean—Hrólf—Helgi. Bjorn buna—Helgi—Helgi—Eyvind eikikrók—Hrólf—Helgi. It is evident that we are dealing here with two branches of the same family. It is most fortunate that the general view of Icelandic historians of the thirteenth century concerning the origin of the Icelanders was not to be the death knell for the tradition of the East Scandinavian origin of the Eyfirthing clan.

I do not hesitate to consider the numerous offspring of Bjorn buna as East Scandinavian. According to an old tradition, the grandfathers of both Bjorn buna and of the viking leader Olvir barnakarl from Agthir are said to be laid at rest in the Brœthrahaug (Brothers' Mound) near Glaumstath in Halland (Sweden). Testimony to this effect is given by Kári, a kinsman of the skald Thjóthólf of Hvinir. It is from the Hvinis-fjord that Bjorn Hrólfsson and his son Eyvind started their expedition west across the North Sea. When they gave up their former homes in Sweden, they had resort to their kinsmen and countrymen who before had helped in the outfitting of their warships from Agthir. In that company Bjorn and his son became the leaders. Now it is quite easy to understand how it is that the skald Thjóthólf of Hvinir shows himself to be so remarkably well informed about early Swedish history: He lived among East Scandinavians. Whether he himself was one of them we shall leave undecided for the present.

During the latter part of the ninth century most of the viking families reside west of the North Sea, including the branches of the family of Hrólf from Ám, of Bjorn buna, and of Olvir barnakarl, likewise kinsmen of the Earls of Mœr and the descendants of King Hjorleif the Uxorious. We are concerned here only with the clans which play a role in the history of Iceland. There were numerous friendships and relationships between these families, which leads one to surmise a common origin for them all. About the time when the colonization of Iceland was beginning, Ketil Flatnose, the father of Auth the Deep-minded and Bjorn the Easterner, was lord over the Hebrides. About the same time the Earls of Mœr achieved domination in the Orkneys. Thorstein Ólafsson, called the Red, the son of Ketil Flatnose's daughter, is termed a warrior-king, just as is Geirmund heljarskinn. Thorstein was the brother-in-law of Helgi the Lean; and Hámund, Geirmund's brother, was the son-in-law of Helgi. No doubt there was an alliance for military exploits between these closely related men. Snorri Sturluson tells us that Thorstein the Red and Earl Sigurth, the brother of Rognvald, Earl of Mœr, became allies and subjugated a large part of northern Scotland. The account of the alliance of the kinsmen of Bjorn buna and the earls of Mœr finds remarkable support in a statement of the authors of the Book of Settlements, as follows: Thórth illhugi, the son of Eyvind eikikrók, a kinsman of Thorstein the Red, "became ship-wrecked on the Breithár Sands,"[8] and Hrollaug, a son of Earl Rognvald of Mœr, gave him land. Four other men are mentioned there who wished to settle on the landtake of Hrollaug, and to them he sold parcels of his land. Thórir snepil, who had been of the company of

[8] *Ldn.* § 361.

Turf-Einar, a brother of Hrollaug, established himself on a piece of land very close to Helgi the Lean. "Skagi Skoptason, a man prominent in Mœr, on the advice of Helgi, took the northerly shore of the Eyjar-fjord, from Varthgjá to the Fnjoskádale River."[9] His land and that of Thórir snepil were contiguous. Dýri was the name of a man who sailed from South Mœr, following the advice of Earl Rognvald. He "gave" Thórth Víkingsson, the brother-in-law of Helgi the Lean and of Thor-stein the Red, a part of his landtake in the Dýrafjord. Eystein the Stout and Molda-Gnúp, both from Mœr, settled in the same neighborhood as did Ketil fíflski (the Foolish), a male cousin of Thorstein. We have not yet mentioned among the settlers another man from Mœr, Thorbjorn súr, who about the middle of the tenth century accepted land from Véstein the Easterner. Véstein himself had obtained a portion of his land from that of Dýri.

It is natural that those of the immigrants who arrived after all the land had been taken up would try to settle in the neighborhood of relatives or former companions if there was a chance to do so. The choice of habitations made by the men from Mœr and the kinsmen of Thorstein the Red is an excellent example of this, more particularly so when we consider the account of Snorri about the alliance of Thorstein and the earls of Mœr.[10] Here, once more, the East Scandinavian antiqui-ties stand us in good stead. This time it is the six chapes which Håkon Shetelig regarded as being fashioned according to East Scandinavian style. One is from Lund, the homestead of Thórir snepil, who followed Turf-Einar to the Shetland Islands. Another is from the eastern shore of the Hrútafjord. There, Eystein, the son-in-law of Thorstein the Red, took land "next after Bálki." The third is from the Skutulsfjord, the landtake of Helgi Hrólfsson, the kinsman of Thorstein. The fourth was found on the landtake of Dýri, who sailed to Iceland on the advice of Earl Rognvald. The fifth was unearthed on the homestead of Ólaf feilan, the son of Thorstein the Red, and the sixth, near the farm which

[9] *Ldn.* § 283.
[10] *Ólafs saga helga*, Chapter 96.

undoubtedly is named after Hafr-Bjorn, a son of Molda-Gnúp from North Mœr. Now it is obvious that the style of ornaments for scabbards to which these chapes bear witness was much in vogue among the allies Thorstein the Red and Earl Sigurth or their kinsmen. And let us at the same time remember that the fashion (in the decoration of scabbards) makes itself felt many hundred times more in Iceland proportionally than in Norway if measured by the number of swords from the Viking Age found in both lands.

There is no need to expatiate on the origin of Thorstein the Red. But do there exist any traditions indicating East Scandinavian origin for the earls of Mœr and a subsequent arrival of his kin on the western scene of their activities? There are a-plenty. In Icelandic sources (Ganger) Hrólf, the progenitor of the earls of Rouen, is said to be the son of Rognvald, Earl of Mœr.[11] But the French historian Dudo, who was the first to write the history of that line,[12] assigns his origin to Denmark. Himself a client of the grandson of Hrólf, Dudo ought to have had good knowledge of this essential matter, even though in some respects he falls short of being a reliable historian. For a long time a bitter fight raged between Danish and Norwegian historians about Hrólf's nationality. I shall not enter into that here. But I do wish to state that I cannot see any contradiction between Snorri Sturluson's declaration that Hrólf was the son of Earl Rognvald of Mœr and Dudo's statement that Hrólf's father, whose name is not given by him, was a great chieftain in Denmark. But it does seem that Snorri thinks Earl Rognvald to be a chieftain foreign to Mœr. And about his son Hrólf he says: "He harried much in the Baltic."[13] On the other hand, Dudo states that Hrólf's father ruled over lands both inside Denmark and outside its boundaries. Evidently he was a viking chieftain who had camps in several places. How often has it not happened in history that the same person had sway over two

[11] *Haralds saga hárfagra*, Chapter 24.

[12] *Dudonis S. Quintini Decani De Moribus et Actis Primorum Normaniæ Ducum* [written 1015–1030], in *Mémoires de la Société des Antiquaires*, XXIII (1865), 141.

[13] *Loc. cit.*

nations at the same time or at different times in his career! Precisely this
occurrence was exceedingly common in the days of Earl Rognvald.
The history of the Viking Age is full of instances of this kind. According
to the Icelandic account, the Earl of Mœr took possession of the Orkneys and set over them as chief Earl Sigurth, his brother. He made an
alliance with the son-in-law of the East Scandinavian viking leader from
the Hvinisfjord. But in Iceland, in the Dales District, there was preserved the memory that Thorstein the Red had originally come from
Denmark, like the earls of Rouen according to Dudo. Also, one's mind
reverts to that strange poem by Hornklofi, where he boasts that King
Harald would not look to a Norwegian spouse but "took a Danish
woman." In the Skálda saga (of the Hauksbók version of the Book of
Settlements) it is stated[14] that the poet who speaks so scornfully of
Norwegian women was a kinsman, on his mother's side, of Hrólf
Rognvaldsson.

It remains to consider the origin of the fifth branch of the family that
had the leadership in the viking domination of the Scottish islands
about the time the settlement of Iceland began. According to the
testimony of the authors of the Book of Settlements, Geirmund
heljarskin was the son of Hjor, the son of Hálf, the son of King Hjorleifs-
son of Horthaland. To judge from the number of generations, Hjorleif,
the ancestor of the family, appears to have lived at the beginning of the
eighth century. "Geirmund heljarskin was a warrior king. He harried
on viking expeditions to the west but ruled in Rogaland."[15] On his
journey to Iceland "he was joined by his kinsman, Úlf hinn skjálgi (the
Squinter) and Steinólf the Short, the son of the hersir Hrólf of Agthir
and of Ondótt, the sister of Olvir barnakarl."[16] Still further, there was
in their company Thránd mjóbein from Agthir. It is a good thing to
have these statements of the Book of Settlements about Geirmund's

[14] *Skálda saga, Hauksbók*, ed. Finnur Jónsson and Eiríkr Jónsson (Copenhagen,
1892–1896), p. 445.
[15] *Ldn.* § 162.
[16] *Ibid.*

company. They acquaint us with the fact that there was a close connection between the kinsmen of King Hjorleif of Horthaland and the vikings in Agthir. There are many other instances that point the same way, though we shall not adduce them here. Geirmund's companion, Thránd mjóbein, was the father-in-law of Hrólf, the son of Helgi the Lean who, as an adult, came to Iceland with his father and Hámund heljarskinn. Gull-Thórir, a settler in the Thorskafjord said to have been of Gautish origin, and Thránd mjóbein both married daughters of Gils skeitharnef. He "took possession of the Gilsfjord from Ólafsdale inward, but to the north contiguous with the landtake of Úlf skjálgi."[17] One may suppose that these colonists were old companions or kinsmen. It was in their settlement that Geiri the Easterner sought refuge when he was forced to withdraw from the Lake Mývatn tract. There settled also Ketil ilbreith, the son of Thorbjorn tálkni. Thorbjorn came to Iceland together with Orlyg the Old, the son of Hrapp, first cousin of Bjorn the Easterner. In an old genealogy[18] he is said to be of Swedish origin. Gils skeitharnef belonged to the same family as did the two kinsmen Skjálda-Bjorn and Sléttu-Bjorn, as shown by the naming in that family: Among the ancestors of the several persons called Bjorn, who are stated to be Swedes, occur such names as Thorgils, Ingibjorg, Héthin, Herfinn and Hergrím. Now, Gils' children are named Thorbjorg, Ingibjorg, Héthin, and Herfinn; and the son of Gils' daughter is called Hergils. For himself Geirmund chose the tract lying between that of Steingrím the Short, his companion, and that of Auth the Deepminded, a tract along the Strands to the west, close by Skjálda-Bjorn. It looks as though all the land round about Geirmund was inhabited by East Scandinavians.

The saga of Hálf and Hálf's Warriors is one of the few in the collection *Fornaldarsǫgur Northrlanda* (Sagas of the Olden Times in the Northlands) which contain real remnants of old tradition. It deals with the ancestors of Geirmund heljarskinn. He is referred to at the end of

[17] *Ldn.* § 163, 168.
[18] *Gríms saga lothinkinna*, Chapter 4; *Ketils saga hœings*, Chapter 5.

the saga, where we are told that from his daughter Ýri "a numerous posterity is descended." In this source Geirmund is stated to be the grandson of some king in Scania. That is what might be expected, seeing that so many heroes perform their deeds in the lands surrounding the Baltic. A good example of this is the tale of the flight of Hálf's warriors after the fall in Horthaland of King Hálf, the grandfather of Geirmund heljarskinn. Bárth and Bjorn seek refuge in Sweden with "King Solvi, the maternal uncle of King Hálf. But Útstein sailed to Denmark to join his kinsman, King Eystein."[19] Hrók the Black resorts to King Haki of Scania. Subsequently "King Solvi and King Haki, together with Hrók the Black, and King Eystein with Útstein, muster a fleet and sail to Norway, where they do battle with King Ásmund,"[20] the slayer of King Hálf of Horthaland, his stepson. At the end of this story about the expedition of these kings of the Baltic to Horthaland in order to avenge Hálf, there is a stanza in the saga in which Hálf's warriors seem to be called "the right [or just] judges [or rulers] of the Danes."

To me it is obvious that the saga of Hálf and Hálf's Warriors has its roots in memories of the East Scandinavian viking company in Horthaland. Moreover, it is most tempting to regard the company of Hálf's warriors as a kind of vanguard for the offensive of East Scandinavian vikings against the north and the west. Einhard,[21] a courtier of Charlemagne, informs us that the King of Denmark had a very considerable foothold on the north shore of the Skagerrak at the beginning of the Viking Age. An Anglo-Saxon annalist of the ninth century[22] mentions that the first band of vikings who raided England came from Horthaland. This must have happened toward the end of the eighth century. At the beginning of his account these viking ships are called ships of Northmen from Horthaland. Very likely, Northmen here signifies

[19] *Hálfs saga*, Chapter 14.
[20] *Ibid.*, Chapter 16.
[21] *Annals of Einhard, sub anno* 813.
[22] *Anglo-Saxon Annals*, ed. Charles Plummer (Oxford, 1892), *sub anno* 787.

men from Scandinavia, because right away, as if to reinforce his statement, he adds: "These were the first ships of Danish men to pillage in
England." If my explanation is correct, vikings from Denmark were
about to get a foothold in Horthaland before the viking expeditions to
England were begun. At this juncture the Eddic Lay of Hyndla lends
support to our argument.

There are diverse opinions about the age of *Hyndluljóth*. This much
seems certain, though, that the main matter of the poem is heathen, and
certainly, as Axel Olrik has shown,[23] connected with Horthaland. The
poem deals with the family and origin of Óttar heimski, the son of
Innstein. In the Hálfs saga Innstein is spoken of as the brother of
Útstein, kinsman of King Eystein of Denmark. Innstein must have
fallen with King Hálf. The poem not only traces, in the narrower sense
of that term, the line of Óttar himself, and mentions his kinsmen in
Horthaland, such as Hild, mother of King Hálf, and the kinsmen of
Hortha-Kári, but also gives an account of the origin of the house of
which these noble families are branches. And who then, in the opinion
of the poet of a thousand years ago so well versed in genealogy, who
then is the progenitor of this line? "Hálfdan, the highest [noblest] of the
Skjoldungs."[24] The progenitor of the line is not Norwegian, much less
some hero of the olden times from Horthaland. He is recalled in the
Anglo-Saxon poem of Bēowulf. This authority is much older than the
Lay of Hyndla and has its roots in East Scandinavian song and lore.
And there we find mentioned not only the Skjoldung king Hálfdan,
but also the people, or fragment of a people, called Hálfdanir (Half
Danes)! The progenitor of the line derives his name from the name of
the people. Hálfdan is a figure parallel to that of Kings Dan and Gaut.
And it lies almost in the nature of things that at first it was the line of
Hálfdan who claimed to be descended from him. In all likelihood the
Halfdanes once dwelled in the ancient boundary lands between the
Danes and the Gauts. There, according to the author of the Lay of

---

[23] *Norske oldkvad og sagnkonger: Norsk Historisk tidsskrift*, III (1893), 168 ff.
[24] *Hēah Healfdene, Bēowulf*, l. 57; *Hálfdan hæstr Skjoldunga, Hyndluljóth*, 14.

Hyndla, "east of Bolm," lived the descendants of Hálfdan. From a branch of the race in Bolm must have descended Ragnar lothbrók and King Eystein, kinsman of Innstein.

Actually, it makes little difference here how true to facts we judge the lay to be. Let be that the genealogical information of its author may to a greater or lesser extent be fanciful; before as well as after, the fact remains that his very genealogy is testimony which makes it certain that the kindred of Óttar heimski, the son of Innstein, is East Scandinavian. It is for this reason that the Lay of Hyndla is such a significant source of information. Also, its author touches on a remarkable circumstance in the cultural history of the descendants of Hálfdan. The divinity they revere is the Vanir goddess Freyja. She vouchsafes to say this about Óttar heimski:[25]

> He a high altar made me of heaped stones—
> all glary have grown the gathered rocks—
> and reddened anew them with neats' fresh blood;
> for aye believed Óttar in the ásynjur [goddesses].

The meaning of the skald is clear: Formerly, great honor was paid to Freyja and the goddesses, but now the world has changed. Also, tradition is witness that the descendants of Hálfdan upheld and preserved their belief in the *dísir*. One may point to the well-known traditions of *dísir* worship in the Víga-Glúms saga[26] and the *thátt* about Thithrandi, whom the *dísir* killed.[27] Memories of these traditions were preserved by the branch of the family from Vors in Horthaland which was related to the kin of Hortha-Kári. The characteristic traits of that family agree excellently with the statement of the poet about the belief in the goddesses within the circle of Óttar heimski's kin and the stanzas in the Hálfs saga where we are told that Útstein, Óttar's paternal uncle,

[25] Stanza 10.
[26] See Chapters 5, 9, 19, 26.
[27] *Thithranda tháttr og Thórhalls*, Chapter 2.

and his kinsmen are worshippers of the *dísir*. It is no accident that Óttar's mother is in the poem plainly called Hlédís the Priestess. She was the woman priest officiating at the stone altar dedicated to Freyja. This may also be the case with the priestess Thorlaug, the wife of Odd Ýrarson. Strong similarities point to her inheriting the office of Ýr, her mother-in-law, who was the daughter of Geirmund heljarskinn. Let us remember that Ýr's sons had a sire of the royal race. Nevertheless, both are named after their mother. Children and farms were apt to be named after women who officiated publicly at sacred functions. We are told in the Book of Settlements that "kinsmen" of Auth the Deep-minded in the Hvamm tract had a "stone altar" made "when sacrifices began."[28] Among them officiated Frithgerth the Priestess. In that clan it was quite customary that children were named after their mother. Hervor was the name of the ancestress of Auth the Deep-minded, and she must have been of royal descent. The name of Hervor is hereditary in that branch of the line of Hálfdan which is associated with Bolm, and nowhere is the name of Auth found except in that line. The Hervarar saga deals with this family. There we find the most detailed information about the worship of Freyja. We consider it worth noting that in those *fornaldar sagas* which preserve remnants of old tradition the memories of Freyja worship are connected with the Horthaland genealogy and the Bolm kin. "Thy sib all these, silly Óttar," as says the author of the Lay of Hyndla.

Geirmund was the son of Hjor, and he, the son of King Hálf, who was again the brother of Hjorólf. Geirmund had three daughters, Geirríth, Ýr, and Arndís, and a brother, Hámund. These names of Geirmund's closest kinfolk scarcely occur in Norway after Iceland was settled. On the other hand, most of them do occur in the ancient history of Sweden. In West Bleking, but a short distance from Scania, there was found a rune stone from the seventh century with the name Hálf Hjorólfsson on it. These names seem most remarkable when we remember that the author of the Hálfs saga has Geirmund heljarskinn claim

[28] *Ldn.* § 147.

descent from Scania and that his forefathers had close associations with chieftains in Baltic lands. Still more noteworthy is the name of his daughter, Arndís. In the Book of Settlements three women bear that name in heathen times. One was the ancestress of Sléttu-Bjorn from Sweden. Of the other two, one was the daughter of the settler Steinolf the Short, who came to Iceland in the company of Geirmund, and the other, the daughter of the Frey worshipper, Thorkel the Tall of Grænavatn. It is clear whence this name, altogether unknown in Norway, came to Iceland. The women's names which have the suffix *-dís* are definitely characteristic of the great viking families which had the leadership in the viking expeditions to the West in the latter part of the ninth century. And they are characteristic especially of the kinsfolk of the companions of Thorstein the Red and Earl Sigurth. We need not have depended on Dudo's account or that of the Laxdæla saga, or on the testimony of the antiquities either, to suspect their East Scandinavian origin. E. H. Lind[29] distinguishes fifteen groups of *-dís* names common in Iceland. Only four of these occur in Norway, and none of them has a wide spread there. Together with skaldic culture, these names in *-dís* vanished in Norway when Iceland was colonized. And this was to be expected. Skaldship and *-dís* names are clearly associated in old Icelandic chieftainly families. Take, for example, the descendants of Thorstein the Red, the Vatnsdæla kin, the sib of the people of Mýrar, and the branch of Saurbæings in the Eyjafjord. Of the daughters of the settlers mentioned in the Book of Settlements, fifteen bear a name compounded with *-dís*. Only one of them occurs in the Eastfjord Quarter, and the bearer belongs to the kin of Bjorn buna. I have demonstrated before that a cultural connection must have existed between the *saur-* farms of our country and the ancient skaldic culture of Icelanders. Now the opportunity is afforded to test the validity of this assertion anew. If there was a connection between the *-dís* names and the culture in which skaldship thrived, then we should, for the first

[29] *Norsk-isländska dopnamn och fingerade namn från medeltiden* (Uppsala, 1905–1915).

*The Origin of the Icelanders*

century of the colonization, expect to find proportionally more -*dís* names in the *saur-* farm districts than in other sections of the country. We shall now enumerate the daughters of the first settlers who, according to the Book of Settlements, bore -*dís* names, and also the tracts in which their fathers dwelled to begin with. We follow the order of districts as given in the register of farms of 1847:

1. Thordís, daughter of Thórth illhugi, Borgarhafna Parish in the East Skaptafells District.
2. Valdís, the daughter of Jólgeir, Holtamanna Parish in the Rangárvalla District.
3. Thordís, the daughter of Thorkel bjálfi, Holtamanna Parish in the Rangárvalla District.
4. Aldís, the daughter of Ófeig grettir, Gnúpverja Parish in the Árness District.
5. Bergdís, daughter of Geir the Wealthy, Reykholtsdal Parish in the Borgarfjord District.
6. Thordís, the daughter of Thorfinn the Stern, Alptaness Parish in the Mýrar District.
7. Thordís, the daughter of Ingvar, Alptaness Parish in the Mýrar District.
8. Thordís, the daughter of Thórhadd, Hraun Parish in the Mýrar District.
9. Halldís, the daughter of Erp, Mithdala Parish in the Dala District.
10. Arndís, the daughter of Steinólf the Short, Saurbæjar Parish in the Dala District.
11. Thordís, the daughter of Thorbjorn súr, Thingeyrar Parish in the Ísafjarthar District.
12. Thordís, the daughter of Ingimund the Old, Ás Parish in the Húnavatns District.
13. Herdís, the daughter of Thórth, Hofs Parish in the Skagafjarthar District.
14. Vígdís, the daughter of Authun rotinn, Saurbæjar Parish in the Eyjafjarthar District.
15. Arndís, the daughter of Thorkel the Tall, Skútustatha Parish in the South Thingeyjar District.

Among the parishes of our land, two are known as Saurbær. Both are distinct from the other thirteen parishes just enumerated. It is well known that the *saur-* farms in these two parishes were established by Authun, the father of Vígdís, and Steinólf the Short, the father of Arndís. This is quite significant. Seven of the 15 -*dís* names occur in the *saur-* farm parishes, and these number only 26, as against 141 other parishes in Iceland. Thus the first-named group of parishes has proportionally almost five times more -*dís* names than the latter. I dare say that the same is true in the case of the court skalds: Of 28 of whose domiciles we are sure, about half by careful count are found to be from *saur-* farm neighborhoods. Forthwith a beautifully clear view opens on the course of development of Old Norse skaldship and at the same time of Icelandic nationality.

It is not by chance that the priestess of Freyja also was called Vanadís. The words *dís* and *gythja* both signify divine beings as well as a woman priest. In the families which attended to the public rituals the professional title of *dís* gradually became the baptismal name, with the most varied first elements added, such as Álf, Arn, Ás, Berg, Ey, Frey, Geir, Hall, Her, Jó, Óthin, Sal, Vé, Víg, Thór, and especially in such families which in ancient times dwelled in *saur-* farm settlements. It is for this reason that by half more woman -*stathir* farms are found there than in other neighborhoods. One may almost assert that the position of women in -*dís* families was on the whole higher than was general with womenfolk, more especially that of the priestesses themselves. From the many stories about swine in *saur-* farm neighborhoods one could infer that there was a close connection between *saur-* and Freyja worship, at least that the *saur-* farms were sacred places for fertility worshippers. Steinólf the Short, who established a saurbær farm was the grandfather of Thórth, the son of Arndís; and Authun rotinn, who at first lived at Saurbær in the Eyjafjord District, was the grandfather of Eyjolf, the son of Valgerth. It all points to the same thing: The mothers of Eyjolf and Thórth, Valgerth, mistress at Saurbær, and Arndís the Wealthy, both were priestesses for the *saur-* worshippers.

Least of all should it now cause any surprise that the skalds of old more often than others were named after their mothers. They were generally members of -*dís* families. With the association of skaldship and the -*dís* names in mind it is possible to explain this singular circumstance: The -*dís* names bear witness to the fact that among the forebears of the first settlers there were families with woman priests. And the performance of public rituals was hereditary in the same family, generation after generation, just as was later the *gothi*dom in Iceland. With that we come to a most important point in pre-Old Norse cultural history: Among a people living under such conditions cultural leadership came to be in the hands of few powerful families which formed a spiritual upper class. On the other hand, no such cultural aristocracy arose in those Scandinavian countries where the heathen congregations themselves performed the sacrifices. The cultural connections between the singular Old Icelandic constitution and skaldship are evident and indubitable. In them is contained the dependable testimony to our people's being older than the colonization of Iceland. Snorri Sturluson says that the Æsir came to the Northlands from the region about the Black Sea under the leadership of twelve temple priests who "have charge of sacrifices and judge between men."[30] Óthin is the highest among them. After great victories and conquests, this tribe, headed by temple priests, journeyed to Denmark and then moved to Sweden. "Óthin instituted such laws as had been in force among the Æsir before." He taught the sacrificial priests most of his skills, and they were nearest to him in all knowledge and magic. His skills "he taught with the runes and songs which are called magic songs [incantations]. For this reason the Æsir are called workers of magic." Óthin and the temple priests have also the name of "songsmiths, because this skill began with them in the Northlands."

It is, then, Snorri's opinion that Norse skaldship and runic culture are inherited from a newcomer tribe and that this tribe abides by the foresight and leadership of temple priests who have preserved and added to this inheritance. It may well be that this view of history leans first and

[30] *Ynglinga saga*, Chapter 6 f.

foremost on memories of the distinctive features of Iceland in the matter of culture and mode of government in saga times. But it is most remarkable that Snorri should assume a particular Norse culture as originating in the distant lands of the Black Sea by the mouth of the River Don. We know that at one time this was the home of a Scandinavian people. They were the Herúli, who are frequently mentioned in writings of the period of the Migration of Nations. Famous scholars like Sophus Bugge[31] and Otto von Friesen[32] think that the knowledge of Runes was brought from the Black Sea to Scandinavia by the Herúli. Early in the sixth century bands of the Herúli under the leadership of chieftains settled in the neighborhood of the Gauts. The account of their migration to the North is recorded by the Greek historian Prokopios,[33] who lived at that time. When the question arises about the origin of skaldship, one must look in directions other than only to the people who now inhabit Scandinavia or the Celtic countries.

[31] His view was first proposed in *Norges Indskrifter med de ældre Runer* (Kristiania, 1905, f. Første hefte).

[32] Latest, in *Runorna, Nordisk Kultur*, Vol. VI (1933), pp. 15 f.

[33] Byzantine historian (500–*ca.* 555). His *Historikon* was written before 553. The migration of the Herúli to the North is described in Book vi. 15. 4.

# 6. Skalds, Ring Swords, Hildisvín

At Saurbær farm on the Hvalfjarthar Strands beldam Skroppa transformed herself and her two daughters into swine.[1] The brother of the
two sisters' grandfather, Hrothgeir the Gentle, had built this Saurbær
farm. Halli the White, the son of a daughter of Helga, the first mistress
at Saurbær in the Eyjafjord, had a home-fed boar which was "so fat it
could scarcely get on its feet." Helgi the Lean, her father, put two swine
on the land when he landed at Galtarhamar (Boar's Cliff). "Three
years later they were found in Solvadale, and they then numbered
seventy swine." From Steinólf the Short, who established Saurbær farm
in the Saurbær Settlement, "three swine" disappeared. About these a
similar story is told. It is not unexpected that these accounts about
swine were preserved in the families who lived in Saurbær farms. Of
fourteen stories about swine from the time of the Settlement and the
Saga Age, nine prove to be associated with Saurbær parishes. Six of
these are located in the neighborhoods of Helga, Steinólf, and Hróthgeir the Gentle. One may call this very astonishing.

The Saurbær farms of Helga, Steinólf, and Hróthgeir stand out in
this respect that the first occupants or owners are known to us. Here
the stories about swine and the many *Hróth-* names of the landtakers are
so closely interrelated that it is impossible to be mistaken. Hróthgeir the
Gentle was the first one to live at Saurbær. Hrólf is the name of Helga's
brother there. Steinólf the Short is the son of Hrólf. Likewise, all Saurbær families have *Hróth-* names in their domain at the time the land was
first occupied. Let be that the examples are few. There is no chance to
be mistaken in this matter. An examination of the names occurring in

[1] For this and the following quotations, see pp. 51–52, notes 15–19.

the Book of Settlements will dispel all doubt. Below is a list of all colonists who bore *Hróth-* names or had a father or son with such names. The *Hróth-* names occurring in the *saur-* farm parishes are easily recognizable:

Hróald bjóla, a settler in the Vápnafjord.
Hróald, father of Eirík, a settler at Hof in Gothdales.
Hróald, the son of Eirík in Gothdales.
Hróald, the son of Hrollaug, a settler at Breithabólstath.
Hróald, the son of Hoskuld, a settler in Skarth.
Hróald, the father of Hof-Kolli, a settler in the Kollafjord.
Hróald, the son of Lothmund, a settler in Sólheimar.
Hróald, the son of Úlf, a settler in Geitland.
Hróar, the father of Onund bíld, a settler in Onundarholt.
Hróar, the son of Hoftha-Thórth, a settler in Hofthi.
Hróar, the father of Sléttu-Bjorn, a settler at Sléttu-Bjarnarstathir.
Hróar, the son of Uni the Dane, a settler.
Hróthgeir the White, a settler in Skeggjastathir.
Hróthgeir the Gentle, settler in Saurbær.
Hróthmar, the father of Hjorleif, a settler.
Hrólf the Stout, a settler in Statharsveit.
Hrólf Helgason, a settler at Gnúpufell.
Hrólf, the father of Kolgrím, a settler at Ferstikla.
Hrólf, the father of Steinólf the Short, a settler in Saurbær.
Hrólf, the father of Molda-Gnúp, a settler in Alptaver.
Hrólf the Redbeard, a settler at Foss.
Hrólf, the son of Úlf, a settler at Geitland.
Hrollaug, a settler at Breithabólstath.
Hrolleif, a settler in Hrolleifsdale.
Hrolleif, a settler in Heithabær.
Hrómund, the son of Eyvind sorkvir, a settler in Blondudale.
Hrómund, a settler in Thverárhlíth.

This list is most remarkable. It contains seven kinds of *Hróth-* names: Hróald (<Hróthvald), Hrólf (<Hróthulf), Hróthmar, Hrollaug (<Hróthlaug), Hrómund (Hróthmund), Hrolleif (<Hrothleif), and

finally Hróar and Hróthgeir, which actually are the same name, Hróar being "derived from Hróthgeir," according to E. H. Lind's excellent book of names.[2] Only Hrólf and Hróar (Hróthgeir) occur in the *saur*-farm neighborhoods. Altogether there are thirteen of these names, or scarcely half of the *Hróth*- names in the list of the Book of Settlements. Eight of them occur in the *saur*- farm parishes, of which there are 26, but only 5 in all the other 141 parishes of our land. Thus skalds, *dísir*, stories about swine, and -*stathir* farms with women's names as their first element have shown themselves as characteristic of the *saur*- farm settlements. And now this curious fact (about *Hróth*- names) must be added to this most remarkable circumstance. Yet is it easily explained. With some attention to Old English epic poems, together with ancient legends and genealogies of Iceland, we may assuredly find the explanation of the riddle.

In the Old English poem Wīdsīth, recognized as the oldest of all Germanic epic poems now known, are mentioned kinsmen of Hróth-úlf and Hróthgeir, a son of a brother, and a paternal uncle, who long were friends after destroying the power of Ingjald and expelling the kin of the Víkings. More is told about these men in Bēowulf. There it is quite clear that Hróthúlf (Hrólf) and Hróthgeir (Hróar) are Skjoldungs and kings of the Danes. Their progenitor is Skyld, who is said to have come to Denmark over the sea as a child. His grandson is Healfdene the Tall, known to us from the Lay of Hyndla as Hálfdan, the Highest (or Most Excellent) of the Skjoldungs. His sons are Hróthgár (Hróar) and Hálga (Helgi), the father of Hrólf. These three Skjoldung kings are dealt with in the Hrólfs saga kraki. King Hróar's queen is Wealtheow (Icelandic Valthjóf) in Bēowulf, and their daughter, Freawaru, who was married to the Hathbarth king Ingjald, the son of Fróthi, who was mentioned above.

Now, it is well known that our forefathers regarded King Ingjald as of Skjoldung race. Two leading Icelandic families trace their ancestry to

[2] See also Assar Janzén, *Personnamn, Nordisk Kultur*, Vol. VII (Stockholm, 1947), pp. 79 f.

him, the Hvammverjar in the Dales, and the Eyfirthings. The author of
the Laxdæla saga represents King Ólaf the White as the son of Ingjald,
the son of Fróthi. And in the Book of Settlements we read this account:
"Bjorn was the name of a person of high birth in Gautland. He was the
son of Hrólf from Ám. His wife was Hlíf, a daughter of Hrólf Ingjaldsson, son of King Fróthi."[3] The son of Bjorn and Hlíf was Eyvind the
Easterner, the defender of the country for Kjarval, King of the Irish,
and the father of Helgi the Lean. Among the children of Helgi the Lean
were Ingjald of Thverá, Helga, mistress in Saurbær, and Hrólf at
Gnúpufell. And the last-mentioned was the father of Ingjald, Bothvar
Valthjóf, and Guthlaug in Hleithrargarth farm.

Even if there were no other evidence than the farm name Hleithrargarth, that would give us a reason for suspecting that the traditions of
the Skjoldungs were familiar to the many offspring of Helgi the Lean.
But as is generally known, King Hrólf kraki and his kinsmen must have
dwelled in Hleithrargarth on the Island of Seeland. Now let us look at
the names in the family of Helga at Saurbær farm: Hrólf, her brother,
is the namesake of Hrólf kraki, the son of Helgi. His sons bear the same
names as King Ingjald, the son of Fróthi, and Bothvar bjarki, the chief
champion of Hrólf kraki. His third brother is called Valthjóf, and thus
has a name like that of Queen Wealtheow. According to Saxa's
account, Hrólf kraki's sister, Bothvar bjarki's wife, had the name Ruta.
Axel Olrik has shown[4] that this is a corruption of the woman's name
Hrút. Parallel to it is the man's name of the same form. Here in Iceland
it occurs only in the line descended from Thorstein the Red, the son of
King Ólaf the White, and his wife, Thuríth, the sister of Helgi the
Lean. Their daughter's son was Hrút Herjólfsson.

Of the kings of old who bore the name *Hróth-*, the kinsmen Hróar
Hálfdanarson and Hrólf kraki were by far the most powerful in legend
and lays. About Hrólf kraki, Snorri Sturluson says that "he was the
noblest of all kings of old, first in generosity, bravery, and condescen-

[3] *Ldn.* § 264.
[4] *The Heroic Legends of Denmark* (1919), Chapter 2, no. 4.

sion."[5] In the epic of Bēowulf, Hróar is the powerful and noble Skjoldung king. Now it is eminently clear why these names especially should characterize the *saur-* farm settlements at the time of the colonization. The reason lies in the fact that men lived there who preserved the age-old traditions of their family and held especially the Skjoldung kings in high honor. We touched on this having been the case in the family of Helga and her brother at Saurbær and of Hrólf at Gnúpufell farm. And now let us dwell a little on the four men in the name list who bear the name Hróar.

First, Hróar, the father of Onund bíld of Onundarholt farm, half brother of Thorgrím bíld at Bíldsfell. Alexander Bugge[6] rightly pointed out that these brothers probably arrived in Iceland from the West. Hróar is said to be the son of the Brúni "who performed a feat in the Battle of Brávoll." This Brúni we hear more of in the Saga Fragment about Kings of Old.[7] Here we are told about the "Skjoldungs" Ívar víthfathmi, Harald hilditonn, and Sigurth Ring, the father of Ragnar lothbrók. Brúni is the leader of the forces of King Harald hilditonn in the Battle of Brávoll. Before the battle he informed the King that Sigurth Ring had drawn up his army in a phalanx formation. But that stratagem Harald thought he alone knew, together with Óthin, and believed it was an evil portent if Óthin had turned against him. In the battle Brúni felled King Harald with a blow of his club. The legend is reliable evidence that the Brúni "who in the Battle of Brávoll performed a feat" is none other than Óthin himself. Now one might think that the genealogy of Onund of Onundarholt farm had very little historical value. But on closer investigation it turns out differently. When tracing the genealogies of the Hvammverjar in the Dales District and the people of Saurbær in the Eyjafjord region back to King Ingjald Fróthason, as was done above, we observe a clear parallelism, and this brings out the important fact that the two branches of this

---

[5] *Skáldskaparmál*, Chapter 41.
[6] *Norges Historie* (Kristiania, 1910), I, 102.
[7] *Sǫgubrot af fornkonungum*, Chapter 9.

line better than other families preserved and glorified their traditions of descent from the Skjoldungs.

The next on our list is Hróar, the son of Hoftha-Thórth, a settler, and of Frithgerth, the granddaughter of Kjarval, king of the Irish. We shall have to keep in mind that kinsmen of this Hróar had been among the Norse vikings in Ireland about and after the middle of the ninth century. In the Sturlubók version of the Book of Settlements his genealogy is stated as follows: Hoftha-Thórth "was the son of Bjorn byrthusmjór, the son of Hróald hrygg, the son of Bjorn járnsítha, the son of Ragnar lothbrók."[8] Again we meet the same strange circumstance: The name of Hróar, the son of Hoftha-Thórth, is likewise found to be linked with the Skjoldung traditions. The same is true of the third Hróar on our list, who is the father of Sléttu-Bjorn, a neighbor of Hoftha-Thórth. Sléttu-Bjorn's line goes back to King Eirík in Uppsala. This King Eirík and Ragnar lothbrók are in the Hervarar saga[9] said to be of the kin of King Ívar víthfathmi. Stories about swine are linked with Ragnar in a most unique fashion. When King Ella took Ragnar prisoner, the latter did not reveal who he was. Then Ella had him cast into a snake tower, and when the snakes had fastened themselves "on him on all sides," Ragnar said: "Grunt now would the shoats if they knew what the old one suffered." "And though he said that, they did not know for sure that it was Ragnar rather than some other king. Then he spoke a verse," which begins with these words:

> Grunt would the shoats
> if they guessed the boar's straits.

This legend is found in the saga of Ragnar lothbrók and his sons.[10] In this saga Hoftha-Thórth is particularly mentioned as a kinsman of Ragnar's; and in this source he alone of all Icelanders shares that honor.

Last, we are bound to recall the lineage of Hróar, the *gothi* of Tunga,

[8] *Ldn.* § 255.
[9] *Hervarar saga*, Chapter 16.
[10] *Ragnar saga lothbrókar og sona hans*, Chapter 15.

son of Uni the Dane. Concerning Uni's sire, the Hauk Erlendsson
version of the Book of Settlements has this to say:[11] "A certain man
was hight Garthar, the son of Svavar the Swede. He owned properties
in Seeland but was born in Sweden." It certainly must arouse our
attention that kinsmen of the fourth generation bearing the name
Hróar are said to be of East Scandinavian origin. Moreover, it is to be
observed that before the introduction of Christianity, no other men
occur in Icelandic history who bear the name Hróar. We perceive the
influence of the Skjoldung traditions also in the environment of the
family of Hróar, the *gothi* of Tunga. On the landtake of his father is a
farm of the same name as the one of Guthlaug, the daughter of Hrólf
of Gnúpufell. Other farms named Hleithrargarth are not known in
Iceland. I do not hesitate to consider both farms named after the famous
Hleithrar of the Skjoldung kings which Icelanders frequently called
Hleithrargarth. How could it be otherwise? The first mistress in the
Eyjafjord Hleithrargarth is thought to be of Skjoldung kin, and the
Eastfjord farm of that name is located in the landtake of the one man
among the settlers who bore the surname of the Dane and appears to
have been brought up in Seeland. With the above instances in mind, I
permit myself to consider it true that here in Iceland the names Hrólf
and Hróar have their origin in the Skjoldung traditions. Any other explanation is hardly possible.

Axel Olrik has shown[12] that the matter of the saga of Hrólf kraki
was influenced by Celtic legends before it was brought to Iceland. It
appears that it was the landtakers of the *saur-* farm settlements, men like
Helgi the Lean, Hoftha-Thórth, and Uni the Dane, who brought this
wealth of legendary material across the sea. Naturally, it is most
reasonable to suppose that it was descendants of the Skjoldung line who
preserved longest and best memories of the kings of that race. And, of
course, most likely those families who came to Iceland by way of
Celtic lands appear to have belonged to the descendants of Hálfdan the

[11] *Ldn.* § 3.
[12] *The Heroic Legends of Denmark*, Chapter 5, no. 2.

Old. Among them one may mention the offspring of Bjorn buna, of Olvir barnakarl, of King Hjor, of Eyvind the Easterner, and of Ólaf the White. They all had camps in the Hebrides and in Ireland around and after the middle of the ninth century, but also at the same time had possessions and kinsmen in Norway. One must suppose that the settlers of lower rank who came to Iceland by way of the British Islands were in the viking companies of these leading families, and so most likely of the same stock. In this connection a sentence in the Hauksbók version of the Book of Settlements about Garthar Svavarsson is very worthy of our attention: "He sailed to the Hebrides in order to fetch the paternal inheritance of his wife."[13] This statement can hardly be explained in any other way than that the Seeland land owner of Swedish stock expected to find in the Hebrides kinsmen and companions likely to let him have the protection of the laws to safeguard his rights and maintain his claim to the inheritance.

The sources agree that Ketil Flatnose, the son of Bjorn buna, was at that time the ruler of the Hebrides. This, according to Håkon Shetelig,[14] must have been before the time King Harald Fairhair took over the government of Norway. It looks as though the kinsmen of Bjorn buna were about to get a foothold in the islands a little before the middle of the ninth century. Orlyg the Old, the nephew of Ketil, and Helgi the Lean were being brought up there, and both migrated to Iceland with their full-grown children. These could hardly have been born after 850. Helgi's mother was Rafarta, a daughter of Kjarval, king of the Irish. She gave birth to the boy in the Hebrides, and he was brought up there the first two years. After that he grew up in Ireland. With Kjarval, his father-in-law, was Eyvind the Easterner, who functioned as the defender of his realm. Now we are at the point which gives us a clear indication of the nationality of the men who brought the Skjoldung traditions to Iceland.

The descendants of Helgi the Lean and of Hoftha-Thórth are not the only ones who traced their lineage to King Kjarval. Five families of

[13] *Ldn.* § 3.        [14] *Det norske folks liv og historie* (Oslo, 1930), p. 188.

Icelandic settlers trace their origin to him. He thus occupies a particular place of honor in the ancient history of Iceland, whereas only three families of landtakers trace their ancestry to Ragnar lothbrók, although many legends about him were current of old. All scholars are agreed that Kjarval, king of the Irish, is identical with Cearbhall, who was king in Ossory, South Ireland, during the years 847–888. Many Celtic kings are known from this time who had dealings with Norsemen, yet no one of them plays a role in Icelandic history except Cearbhall. This is a more important circumstance than has been suspected, and there is only one explanation for it: The settlers who came from Ireland and the new Hebridean viking colony had a closer and better knowledge of Cearbhall than of any other Celtic prince. The veracity of some families tracing their origin to him may be doubtful. But that makes no difference in this connection.

Now we are in the extraordinarily fortunate position of having Irish sources state clearly what was the nationality of the Norse vikings who were in the service, or were confederates, of Cearbhall about the time Eyvind the Easterner must have been with him: *They were Danes.* About 850 they won Dublin from the Norwegians, and thereupon fought that fierce battle against the Norwegians in that locality. The Danish vikings then allied themselves with Cearbhall. The king received them with marks of great honor and "gave them help against the Norwegian vikings." Thereafter the Danes were "frequently in the army of the king when he was victorious over the foreigners," as says our Irish source.[15] In the judgment of Jan de Vries,[16] this alliance lasted for many years: "The men of Ossory were in steady conflict with the Norwegian vikings and had the support of the Danes." Thus it is quite evident that those men who honored the name of Cearbhall most highly and traced their lineage to him were descendants of those Danish or East Scandinavian vikings from Ossory and Dublin. It is

[15] *Annals of Ireland: Three Fragments,* ed. John O'Donovan (Dublin, 1860), pp. 115 ff.
[16] *Norsk historisk tidsskrift,* 5 række, Vol. V (1924), 515.

another matter that these vikings often were apt to sail west across the sea from their camps on Norwegian shorelands. That was exactly the case with Eyvind the Easterner, the man from Gautland, who is stated to be of Skjoldung descent.

So there is no need to wonder why our old skalds and saga writers had better knowledge of East than of West Scandinavian traditions of the olden times: They themselves were East Scandinavians from generations back. This may be best illustrated with the tales of swine in our old literature. The overlord of both the Swedes and the Danes, Harald hilditonn, thought that he alone knew how to draw up his forces in a phalanx formation. "Grunt would the shoats now if they knew what their sire suffered"—that must be an expression or watchword characterizing Ragnar lothbrók, so that he could be told apart from other kings. He is, moreover, made to call himself a boar, and his sons, shoats. These strange tales would hardly be explicable unless regard were had to the tales about swine connected with the old Skjoldung kings Hrólf kraki and Hróar Hálfdanarson. And there is in these legends a great deal to be gathered about this matter. None of the *fornaldarsǫgur Northrlanda* (Sagas of Ancient Times in the Northlands) contains as many and as remarkable tales about swine as does the saga of Hrólf kraki.[17] When he visits his stepfather, King Athils in Uppsala, he is fiercely attacked by a boar which Athils had sacrificed. Queen Yrsa gives her son Hrólf the ring Svíagrís (Pig of the Swedes). On his flight from Uppsala, Hrólf casts the ring on the ground before King Athils, who pursues him. And when Athils bends down to pick it up, Hrólf exclaims: "Now I made him who is most powerful among the Swedes stoop like a swine." Finally, "a frightful boar" decides the outcome of the battle incited by Queen Skuld against King Hrólf. "Arrows fly from every one of his bristles and kill Hrólf's followers in a monstrous fashion," as says the saga writer. Here it is proper to mention the account given by Snorri Sturluson[18] of the helmet Hildisvín (Battle

---

[17] For the following quotations, see *Hrólfs saga kraka*, Chapters 40–45, 51.
[18] *Skáldskaparmál*, Chapter 41.

Swine). Aided by the champions of Hrólf kraki, King Athils felled
Áli of Uppland and "took from his dead body the helmet Hildisvín
and his horse called Raven. Thereupon the berserkers of King Hrólf
kraki demanded their pay, three pounds of gold for each of them, and
besides they demanded to bring Hrólf kraki the valuables they chose
for him, which were the helmet Hildigolt and the byrnie Finnsleif,
against neither of which iron was effective, and the gold ring called
Svíagrís, which had been in the possession of Athils' forebears."

In the Lay of Hyndla, the poem dealing with the descendants of
Hálfdan the Old, Freya's boar is called Gullinbursti (Golden Bristled)
"which the skillful dwarfs, Dáin and Nabbi, made for me."[19] As with
the other names, it was difficult to explain why helmets came to be
called Hildigolt and Hildisvín. But the matter was explained after
Grímur Thorkelin rescued from oblivion the poem Bēowulf. He was
the first to publish this priceless source, in 1815. In it the poet states that
weaponsmiths had in former times adorned helmets with figures of
wild boars so that they could withstand both sword blows and fire.
From the description of the helmets in the poem one may clearly infer
that these figures of swine were apt to be of gold, and either engraved
on the ornamental border which surrounded the helmet, or else the
figure of a boar was fastened to the crown of the helmet. Helmets like
these appear to have been worn by the *eorlas* (warriors) in the hall of
Hróar Hálfdanarson, and such was the helmet Hildisvín. It has its name
from this sacred and distinctive feature. Poets and saga authors imagined
that Ragnar lothbrók and his kinsmen wore the figure of a swine as a
distinguishing characteristic, and for this reason they are in the saga
called boar and shoats. Parallel to this, possibly the kenning "helm" is
used in Bēowulf time and again for princes, three times, for instance,
for King Hróar.

Hróar Hálfdanarson, Hrólf kraki, King Athils, and Áli of Uppland
most likely were real persons who lived in the sixth century. Four
generations before that, we encounter a tribe which evidently had the

[19] *Hyndluljóth*, stanza 7.

same belief in swine as these men had. This tribe was at that time located on the southeastern corner of the Baltic where the boundary between Lithuanians and Germans is now. The Roman historian Tacitus has this statement:[20] "We must now turn to the righthand shore of the Suebic Sea: here it washes the tribes of the Æstii; their customs and dress are Suebic, but their language is nearer British. They worship the mother of the gods: as an emblem of that superstition they wear figures of wild boars: this boar takes the place of arms or of any other protection, and guarantees to the votary of the goddess a mind at rest even in the midst of foes. They use swords rarely, clubs frequently. Grain and other products of the earth they cultivate with a patience out of keeping with the lethargy customary to Germans: nay, they ransack the sea also, and are the only people who gather in the shallows and on the shore itself the amber, which in their tongue they call glæsum [glass]."

Senior teacher Páll Sveinsson adds the following comment to Tacitus' statement about the mother of the gods and the figures of the swine: "In Norse mythology the boar is sacred to Freyja, and in the consciousness of men she frequently became identical with Frigg, mother of the gods." Like skaldic culture, the belief in swine is firmly linked in the religion of our forefathers with the worship of the Vanir deities. Freyja and the sow both have the name Sýr, Frey and the boar, the name Vaningi. Accompanying both divinities is the boar Gullinbursti or Hildisvín. Now, it is generally known that in the religious life of our forefathers the Vanir gods Njorth, Frey, and Freyja were the successors of the goddess Nerthus, whom Tacitus calls *terra mater* (Mother Earth) and states to have been venerated by seven Germanic tribes.[21] Among these are mentioned the Jutes (Evdoses) and Angles (Anglii), who later migrated to Britain. Of the Germanic tribes both the Æstii (Esthonians) and those who worship Nerthus are ranged by Tacitus with the Suebii. As I see it, the main feature of their religion was of the same nature. At

[20] Tacitus, *Germania*, Chapter 45.
[21] *Ibid.*, Chapter 40.

least, the worship of fertility and veneration of a goddess was character-istic of both at the time of Tacitus.

From Wīdsīth,[22] which is based on age-old tradition, we learn that at one time the Eider River, which separates Holstein from Schleswig, was regarded as the boundary between the Suebi, the Angli, and the Myrgings. In the opinion of the poet, these Suebi were closely related to the Angli. The Myrgings are hardly mentioned anywhere but here. So it is strange that King Athils (Eadgils), famous of old, in the poem is called the chief of the Myrgings. Both Snorri and Saxo relate that he warred on the Saxons as well as on the inhabitants of South Jutland. After the poet has spoken about the great among the Angli, the Suebi, and the Myrgings, he hurries on to make a statement about the kinsmen Hróar and Hrólf and their war against the tribe of the Vikings. This may seem peculiar when we consider that it is precisely these kinsmen and Athils who are dealt with most in the Icelandic traditions about the Skjoldungs. It is they about whom crowd the tales of swine. Hrólf kraki and his stepfather Athils fight about the ring Svíagrís and the helmet Hildisvín, both of which Áli of Uppland had owned. In Bēowulf, Áli appears as Onela, and is there stated to be the paternal uncle of Athils and, it would seem, the brother-in-law of Hróar. There, the ring Sviágrís and the helmet Hildisvín are seen as the choice treasures and symbols of power of the royal house. Also, Snorri Sturluson says about the ring that it had always belonged to the family of Athils. Too, his name points in that direction.

Finds of antiquities have corroborated the statements of our sources about the figures of boars on helmets. None of these finds is later than from the seventh century. It is specifically stated in Bēowulf, a poem assumed to have been composed a little later, that the weaponsmiths had of yore fashioned such helmets. The oldest occurrence of *hildisvín* helmets is seen in the find made at Gundestrup near Hobro, in that part of Jutland which is surrounded by the Limfjord in the north and west. There, in the year 1891, was unearthed a large sacrificial bowl of silver,

22 *Wīdsīth*, ll. 21 f.

richly decorated with figures clearly showing the characteristics of
Celtic art and religion. Among the figures are two representing
warriors wearing boar helmets. According to C. P. Neergaard[23] the
cauldron dates from the first or second century A.D., which would
agree with its having been fashioned about the time Tacitus wrote his
account of the tribes which believed in the protective power of the boar
images and spoke a language closer to a British than a Germanic tongue.
Other antiquities which confirm the statements of the use of helmets
with boar images all date from the sixth or seventh century.

In his monograph on Helmets and Swords in Bēowulf,[24] Knut
Stjerna speaks of the remarkable agreement between the statements of
the poem about the armor and certain kinds of helmets which were in
fashion among the East Scandinavian chieftains, as evidenced by the
antiquities. Besides these ornamental helmets with the figures of boars
and metal borders, we often hear in the poem of the characteristic ring-
swords. They have their name from the ring attached to the upper part
of the hilt. This ring probably was a symbol of the sun and of the sacred
court of justice, as was the altar ring of the Icelandic temple priests
three centuries later. On this kind of ring men swore sacred oaths.
About the end of the sixth and the beginning of the seventh centuries,
men appear to have stopped attaching rings to sword hilts, and at about
the same time the wearing of ornamental helmets went out of fashion
in the North. But as with other things, the memory of these chieftainly
valuables was preserved in Norse legends and poems. To be sure, the
Norse literary monuments are of much later date than Bēowulf. Ring
swords are mentioned in the Lays of Helgi Hjorvarthsson and of Sigurth
Fáfnisbani; and ornamental helmets, in the Lay of Atli and the Lay of
Hloth. Likewise, Thorbjorn hornklofi, in his Lay of Harald, speaks of
"graven helmets." But as Shetelig remarks in his History of Norway,[25]

---

[23] "Gundestrup Karret," in *Salmonsens Konversations Leksikon* (2d ed.; Copenhagen, 1920), X, 423.

[24] Knut Stjerna, *Essays on Questions Connected with the Old English Poem of
Bēowulf* (1912), Chapter 1.

[25] *Det norske folks liv og historie* (Oslo, 1930), p. 156.

"The poetic choice of words harks back to an older time than that of the poet himself." It is clear that in the seventh century a close connection obtained between the customs of wearing helmets adorned with figures and of having rings on sword hilts. In Bēowulf we encounter both, and the custom was obviously associated with the religious beliefs of the time: Ring swords and ornamental helmets have been found in the same grave. On a bronze plate from the early seventh century unearthed on the island of Oland (Sweden) we see the figure of a warrior with a ring sword in his hand and a helmet adorned with a boar on his head. These antiquities suggested to me the idea that it might pay to find out in what kind of legendary connection there appeared in Norse literature statements about ring swords and ornamental helmets.

The first to come to mind are the Eddic legends about Helgi Hjorvarthsson. "Helgi sat on a hill and saw nine valkyries riding past, of whom one was the noblest. That was Sváva, the daughter of Eylimi. She said:

> Swords know I lie/in Sigarsholm,
> a full fifty/but four, I ween.
> Of the bitter brands/the best is one,
> a wound-dealing wand/all wound with gold.

> There's a ring on the hilt, etc.

... Then sought Helgi the sword to which Sváva had directed him."[26]

Hethin, Helgi's brother, "one time was coming home alone from the forest on Yule eve. He met a troll woman riding on a wolf, with snakes as reins. She asked his leave to keep him company, but he would not. She said: 'That shalt thou rue when drinking from the hallowed cup.' In the evening vows were made: the sacrificial boar was brought in, men laid their hands on him and swore dear oaths as they drank from the hallowed cup. Hethin made a vow that he would have Sváva,

[26] *Helgakvitha Hjorvarthssonar*, stanzas 8 f.

Eylimi's daughter, the maiden beloved by Helgi, his brother; but he forthwith rued it so greatly that he hastened South on wild ways till he found his brother Helgi."[27] Here there is no great distance between legends about a ring sword and boar worship.

The sword of Sigurth Fáfnisbani is termed "ring-adorned"; and the sons of Gjúki, his brothers-in-law, were invited to come to the hall of Atli, king of the Huns, with "helmets ring-dight."[28] After they had accomplished Sigurth's death, Guthrún, Gjúki's daughter, seeks consolation and shelter at the Danish court. In the Second (Old) Lay of Guthrún we are told that Grímhild gave her "a goblet to drink./Was the mead mixed with the might of the earth,/with ice-cold sea and the sacred boar's blood."

In the beaker was also "a swine's boiled liver/her sorrow to deaden."[29] The same observation—that ring-dight helmets and swine worship are closely associated—holds about these two legendary accounts as of the former.

A third parallel passage occurs in the Hervarar saga. In the Lay of Hloth (incorporated in it) we find these lines:

> Hloth was born there/in Hunnish lands,
> with short-swords and brands/and byrnie long,
> with helmet ring-dight, etc.[30]

There are three different versions of the legend about the beliefs of King Heithrek. One runs as follows: "King Heithrek used to sacrifice to Frey. The largest boar he could obtain he was wont to give to Frey. They called that boar so sacred that [oaths in] all important suits were to be sworn on his bristles, and that boar was to be sacrificed as an atonement. On Yule Eve the atonement boar was led into the hall before the King. Then the men would lay their hands on his bristles and make

[27] *Ibid.*, 6th Prose.
[28] *Atlakvitha*, stanza 3 (emended).
[29] *Guthrúnarkvitha ǫnnor*, stanzas 21 and 23.
[30] *Hlothskvitha*, stanza 1.

vows."[31] In another version the boar is called *sonargoltr* (sacrificial boar).

Relevant, though of a somewhat different nature from the three instances cited here, since it concerns only ancestors on the sword side and not the family in the narrowest sense of the term, is the statement by Snorri Sturluson about the Yngling king Dag:[32] "He had a sparrow which told him many tidings. . . . One time this sparrow flew into Reithgothaland and to the farm called Vorvi. It flew to the field of a farmer and fed there. The farmer came up and seized a stone and killed the bird. King Dag felt greatly concerned when the sparrow did not return to him. He prepared a sacrifice, offering up a boar to Frey, to find out what had happened, and received the answer that his sparrow had been killed at Vorvi." The Yngling King Athils sacrificed a boar and took the helmet Hildisvín from the dead body of Áli of Uppland. Harald Fairhair presented his courtiers with "graven helmets," as says Hornklofi. It is not unlikely that his choice of words about these helmets is indebted to old lays about the Ynglings. When Harald's ancestors removed themselves from Uppsala, "graven helmets" were customary in those parts.

King Helgi Hjorvarthsson has in his possession a *ring sword*, and his brother Hethin "lays his hands" on the *sacrificial boar* and makes a vow. Sigurth Fáfnisbani owns a *ring sword*, and his wife drinks *sonardreyri* (the blood of sacrifice); her brothers wear ornamental helmets. Hloth has a *skrauthjálm* (ornamental helmet), his father, a *sonargolt* (sacrificial boar). Athils possesses the helmet *hildisvín* which appears to be a treasure belonging to his line. His forefather goes to *sonarblót* (atonement sacrifice). Now I have enumerated the main points of the parallel passages in these legends. On the one hand, there are two ring swords and helmets in the Bēowulf description of the weapon equipment of warriors and the East Scandinavian chieftainly custom of the sixth and seventh centuries. On the other hand, we have four accounts about

[31] *Hervarar saga*, Chapter 10.
[32] *Ynglinga saga*, Chapter 18.

swine, showing consistent characteristics which distinguish them from all other tales about swine in Icelandic literature, viz., the first element of the words *sonarblót, sonardreyri,* and *sonargoltr.* It may seem symbolic that it has not proved feasible to explain these words except by comparison with the language of the Langobardi and Old English. In the days of Tacitus these tribes were neighbors and were counted among the Suebi. The Langobardi called the sacrificial boar *sonarpair,* and in Old English a herd of swine is *sunor.* The great philologist Eduard Sievers[33] considered that the words *sonardreyri* and *sonarblót* have an erroneous form in Norse writings and ought rather be *sonargaltardreyri* (blood of the sacrificial boar) and *sonargaltarblót* (sacrifice of the herd boar).

Though *sonargolt* does not occur as a name among Icelandic swine, yet this select animal is clearly discerned in the stories about them. For a wonderfully long time the tale about a fat home-fed boar was preserved at the farm Jórunnarstathir in the Saurbær Parish before it was written down on the parchment. The leading boars in the swine herds of Ingimund the Old and Helgi the Lean are honored with the names of chieftains famed of old from the times when warriors had hildisvín (the images of "battle swine") on their helmets. They are called Beigath and Solvi. Beigath was the name of one of Hrólf's champions who wanted to regain the helmet Hildisvín and the ring Svíagrís from King Athils. An earl from Jutland by the name of Solvi felled King Eystein and his son and made himself king of Sweden. I have no doubt that there is some connection in this naming. The leader boars Beigath and Solvi were veritable "atonement boars"; but, just like ring swords and helmets adorned with figures, this term was no longer used when Helgi and Ingimund lost their swine. Nevertheless, the belief in swine still flourished at that time in Iceland. Otherwise, tales about swine, together with the practice of the skaldic art, would not have distinguished the *saur-* farm districts in the colonization and the saga periods.

As might be expected, the worship of swine, and also skaldship, were

---

[33] *Paul und Braune Beiträge,* XII, 177; XVI, 540 ff.

associated for a long time among our forefathers in the Northlands
before Iceland was colonized. Neither can be called common to Norse,
let alone Germanic, culture. We saw that Tacitus stated the worship of
swine images as being a characteristic of individual tribes among the
Germani; and his statements show that such a belief was not actually
widespread among Germanic tribes in his days. At the same time, it is
evident from the parallel passages adduced above that the worship of
sacrificial boars and the custom of using ring swords and image-
adorned helmets were associated with one another. Nor is the connection between these customs, on the one hand, and Old English and
Norse poetic language, on the other, less evident. Kennings are characteristic of Old English as well as Norse poetry. Helmets are of exceedingly common occurrence in the kennings. Even God is called "the
helm of heaven" in Bēowulf, and in our own poetry we find helmets in
very many compounds which are to be classed as kennings. Assuredly
the cause for this is to be found in the custom of having sacred figures
like "battle boars" on the helmets. The realistic and exact language the
skalds use for the distinctive features of ornamented helmets and ring
swords shows likewise that among those who wore these treasures,
Norse skaldship thrived in the olden times. Even if this were not so,
archaeology alone would inform us about these matters, and literature
could be as silent as the grave about them.

It is certain that the main matter of Bēowulf derives from East
Scandinavian sources. The same is true of the Ynglingatal and the
heroic lays of the Edda. Those who in the first place used this matter
drew especially on their knowledge of the islands and shores of the
Baltic as well as of the routes in the South to and from the lands of the
Huns and the Goths. The Norse settlements along the Atlantic appear
to be entirely outside the ken of these men. Not a single tradition, and
scarcely any place name, of these poems harks from these regions. And
yet it was the island dwellers in the Atlantic Ocean who preserved this
cultural inheritance and steadily increased it. At the same time, it must
be borne in mind that contemporaneously, when epic poetry began to

flourish in the North, there arose a great difference in the character of the antiquities of West and of East Scandinavian settlements. Various cultural currents from the south and southwest exert their influence on the North. This is seen in the so-called Vendel, or Continental, style, which set its stamp on the fashions in ornaments and on the weapons of East Scandinavian nobles. They are stated to exhibit clear signs of influences from Byzantium and Italy and of having come to the North by way of South Germany. Now, we know with certainty about a Scandinavian tribe which in the Migration Period had close connections with Byzantium and Italy. It was the *Herúli* or *Earls* who, as Otto von Friesen[34] and Sophus Bugge believe, brought the art of writing to the North. Moreover, it is well known that groups of southern Herúli settled at the beginning of the sixth century in the neighborhood of the Gauts.[35] That was at the time of King Hróar Hálfdanarson and of Áli of Uppland. No other migrations of southern tribes to the North are known from classic sources, whether Greek or Roman.

When we speak of the Vendel style and the beginnings of epic poetry in the North, our minds are bound to turn to the Herúli. It is the opinion of von Friesen that they dwelled south of the Skaw and on the Island of Funen till about 500 A.D. In the first centuries A.D. they appear to have lived in the southwest corner of the Baltic in those parts where, according to Tacitus, dwelled the swine worshippers who believed in the "mother of the gods." In the third century the Herúli, together with the Goths, migrated to southern Russia, settling by the shores of the Sea of Azov, east of the seat of the Goths.[36] There, as Snorri Sturluson[37] relates, the Æsir and Vanir gods must have dwelled before they brought the Skaldic culture to the North and there founded a dominion, first on Funen, and later in the Swedish province of Uppland, where are located the famous towns of Uppsala, Sigtúna, and

[34] See p. 121, notes 31 and 32.
[35] Prokopios, *Historikon* vi. 15. 4.
[36] *Ibid.*, vi. 14. 1.
[37] *Ynglinga saga*, Chapters 2–7.

Vendel. From Vendel in Uppland the southern fashion of ornamentation derives its name.

In the year 267–268 a fleet of Herúli from the shores of the Sea of Azov harried in the lands on the Aegean.[38] Hardly a century afterwards the Herúli came under the powerful rule of the East Gothic King Ermanaric,[39] who in the Eddic lays and the Volsunga saga is called Jormunrek. Somewhat later, when the Huns overran the lands by the Euxine, the East Goths had to submit to Hunnish overlordship, and the same appears to have been the fate of the Herúli. Then, on the ruins of the great empire of Attila, there arose, in the latter part of the fifth century, a strong kingdom of the Herúli in the eastern section of Hungary. They took a considerable part in the campaign of Odoacer against Italy in the year 476 and received land there as a reward. Hardly a generation later the Langobards overpowered their kingdom in Hungary. Then it was that some of the Herúli decamped and migrated to the Northlands under the leadership of chieftains of royal birth;[40] while others besought the grace of the East Roman emperor and were permitted to settle in his dominions.[41] During the sixth century thousands of them were in the service of the Byzantine emperors. There is reliable evidence to the effect that during this period connections were maintained between the South and the North Herúli. Their entire history is most remarkable, and especially so when we endeavor to explain the cultural type of the Norse in olden times. It is not at all impossible that Huns, Goths, and their kings Atli and Jormunrek owe the Herúli their fame in northern legend, and we Icelanders, various distinctive features of our culture in times past. But let that main matter wait till the final chapter of our exposition.

Now to revert to the Vendel culture with its ornamental helmets and ring swords. Håkon Shetelig's description of the chief distinctive

[38] According to the Greek historian Dexippos, *Fragmenta Historicorum Graecorum*, III, 680 f.

[39] Prokopios, *Historikon* vi. 15. 1.

[40] *Ibid.*, vi. 15. 4.

[41] *Ibid.*, vi. 14. 34.

features of this period begins thus: "Prototypes of the style are first and foremost animals' heads as independent ornaments, especially crudely made *heads of wild boars* and birds' heads with curved beaks and big eyes."[42] It is by all means pertinent to note where these swords and helmets have been found, at the same time taking account of Norse place names in the Ynglingatal and the Eddic lays. Not counting names of countries, those names, which one can locate with some certainty are: the Limfjord, the Danish islands Hlesey (Læsö), Samsey (Samsö), and Funen; Hleithrar (Leire), the Swedish Eyland (Oland) and Bolm; the Uppland names Uppsala, the Fyrisá River, and Vendel, which gave the style its name; and finally the East Norwegian place names Thótn (Toten), Skíringssal, and a few others in West Fold where kings of the Yngling race were entombed. According to Knut Stjerna's description[43] of helmet fragments, representations of such, and ring swords from the sixth and seventh centuries, the antiquities, some thirty in number, were distributed as follows in the various localities: The province of Uppland in Sweden had twelve, most of them having been found in the famous chieftains' graves near Vendel. Five were unearthed on the island of Gotland, four on Funen, three on Öland. Six were found scattered in the Swedish provinces of Södermanland, Scania, West Gotland, and in the east of Norway, viz., in Totn, Hedemark, and East Fold. About the time he wrote his survey of the location of finds, there had in addition been discovered in West Fold and Hedemark helmet fragments dating from the sixth century. Since then forty years have elapsed. I have not had the opportunity to learn about the locations of similar finds in the last decades. However, they are likely to be few, and there is little chance that the picture of the whole which Stjerna's list shows will differ essentially. In Norway it is the settlements around Lake Mjösen and the Oslofjord which are distinguished by finds of antiquities; in Sweden, Uppland, Gotland, and Öland; and in Denmark, Funen. On Funen, to be sure, only ring swords have been found,

---

[42] *Det norske folks*, pp. 157 f.
[43] See note 24, above.

three of them in the parish of Gudme (Gotheim) in the southeast of the island.

Funen is mentioned in the Second Lay of Guthrún in such a manner that one may infer that age-old legends were connected with that island. The poet has Guthrún state that when grief-stricken, she resided in Denmark with Thóra, the daughter of Hákon, and they weaved representations of events, as for example:

> Seaward sailing,/King Sigmund's ships,
> with golden beaks/and graven stems;
> in the web they weaved/the wars which fought
> Sigar and Siggeir/south on Funen.[44]

It looks as though the matter here is taken from the legend of Sigurth Fáfnisbani and his line, in which the names Sigar, Siggeir, and Sigmund occur. Helgi Hjorvarthsson, who, like Sigurth Fáfnisbani, possessed a ring sword, obtained his on Sigarshólm, as Sváva, the daughter of Eylimi, had directed him. Hjordís, Sigurth's mother, was also a daughter of Eylimi, so this suggests that the dís and the valkyrie were at one time regarded as of the same family or as sisters. At any rate both their fathers bore the name Eylimi, just as Helgi and Sigurth are the only ones in the Eddic lays who possess ring swords. And it is certain that the tradition of Sigar's warfare is associated with the island which has preserved all the Danish ring swords. One suspects that Sigarshólm and Funen are one and the same.

Vendel, and certainly also Eyland (Öland), are clearly referred to in the accounts of the old poems. In the Ynglingatal[45] we learn that "Eyland-earls of Fróthi" had slain King Óttar at Vendel. Many reasons have been adduced to prove that this refers to the Vendel in Swedish Uppland. Óttar was the father of King Athils and the brother of Áli of Uppland. From Athils in the seventh generation must have descended the first Yngling king in Norway, Hálfdan hvítbein. Birger Nerman[46]

[44] *Guthrúnarkvitha ǫnnor*, stanza 16.
[45] *Ynglingatal*, stanza 19.
[46] Birger Nerman, *Studier över Sveriges hedna literatur* (Uppsala, 1913), pp. 205 f.

calculates that he lived at the end of the sixth and the beginning of the seventh centuries. Three place names occurring in the Ynglingatal are connected with Hálfdan: He died at Thótn and was buried in a mound at Skæreith in Skíringssal in South West Fold. According to Snorri Sturluson, Hálfdan rose to power in Norway with the aid of the Swedes who had left their native country for the reason "that there were more people there than the country could sustain."[47] Hálfdan "took possession of much of Heithmork, Thótn, and Hathaland, together with a large portion of West Fold." Here Snorri in the same breath enumerates those three parts of Norway which preserved traces of ornamental helmets in the Vendel style. This remarkable accordance of legend and antiquities is quite easily understood when we consider the distribution of place names in the ancient poetry and the location of the finds of antiquities such as ornamental helmets and ring swords in Scandinavia as a whole. The legends which the Icelandic colonizers knew about the kings and heroes of the Migration Period had their origin in the poetry of those times. Hence the skaldic culture of us Icelanders certainly derives from those whom one must regard as the standard-bearers of the Vendel style in the North. Skalds, ring swords, and battle-swine ornaments of helmets belong together.

[47] *Ynglinga saga*, Chapter 43. The quotation refers, however, to the Swedes who migrated to Värmaland, then to Norway. Hálfdan hvítbein is a scion of the Swedish royal race of the Ynglings.

# 7. The People of Iceland Are Older than the Settlement

In his book *Farms and Fanes of Ancient Norway*, Magnus Olsen discusses the highly remarkable difference between the Norwegian and the Icelandic -*stathir* farm names.[1] According to his count, there are in Norway about 2,500 such, and about 1,100 in Iceland. Olsen calls attention to the fact that more than one-tenth of all Icelandic -*stathir* farms are named after women, as against only about some thirty in Norway, if doubtful instances are reckoned in; and it may be nearer the truth to lower that number by about half. In other words, the Icelandic farms with women's names would proportionally be at least ten times more numerous than the Norwegian ones.

When more than ten years ago my attention focused on this point, it became clear to me that here we had to deal with an uncommonly important phenomenon in the ancient history of Scandinavia. I had by then arrived at the conclusion that there could be no question of the Icelandic settlers' being in the main of Norwegian stock, in the usual sense of the word, even though they came to Iceland from Norway. One becomes aware of great differences in most of the chief aspects of Icelandic and Norwegian culture in ancient times. Thus right from the beginning this is apparent in the dissimilar constitutions of the two countries, in the order of the social classes, and in matters concerning the rights of men. It is clear from the burial customs of Norwegians and Icelanders in heathen times that the religious views of people in Iceland were formed by cultural factors different from those present in the

---

[1] *Farms and Fanes of Ancient Norway* (Oslo, 1928), pp. 115–116.

kindred nation to the east. Once the Age of Settlement had ended, the Icelanders became the leaders in Scandinavia in the field of skaldship. It would appear that this word art and the cultural conditions which fostered it almost disappeared in Norway, together with the emigrants who peopled Iceland.

Olsen's observation directed my thought to the possibility that it might be easy to find here the explanation of this very important fact in the cultural history of the two nations. Already in heathen times Norway was poor in skalds and woman -*stathir* farms, and Iceland rich in both. In case there was a cultural connection between skaldship and woman -*stathir* farms, it would not be inconceivable that traces of this connection might be found in the varied and most extensive supply of source materials in ancient Iceland. I first of all took in hand the very serviceable Register of Farms which Jón Jónsson published in 1847, counted the -*stathir* farms occupied at that time, grouped them according to the nature of the first element in their names, and followed this up with Finnur Jónsson's list of -*stathir* farms in Collections toward a History of Iceland,[2] when it became apparent that those parts the court skalds hailed from proved to have proportionally by half more woman -*stathir* farms than other parts of the country. I limited myself to the court skalds who flourished in the tenth century and the first part of the eleventh.

Taken by itself, the immense difference in the number, in Norway and in Iceland, of -*stathir* farms named after women is hardly capable of explanation unless we proceed on the assumption that of old, Icelandic women enjoyed far greater freedom of action than their sisters in Norway. It is significant already how great a role women play in the Eddic lays and in those traditions from heathendom which are preserved in the Book of Settlements. Time and again we encounter women as independent landtakers in Iceland who at times are even foremost among them. It is also mentioned in the Hauksbók version of the Book of Settlements that particular regulations were in force as to how much

[2] In *Safn til Sögu Íslands* (Copenhagen, 1907–1915), IV, 412–585.

land women could take. If, now, the suspicion is correct that there was a close connection between higher skaldship and the origin of farms named after women, there is good reason to believe that skaldship had thrived especially in those families in which women at one time had the spiritual guidance in their hands, for example, by having charge of the sacrifices and other religious ceremonies. A search for their sanctuaries was therefore made in those parts of the country where -*stathir* farms were most in evidence. So my attention was quickly directed to the *saur*- farms. In those sections in which there were *saur*- farms, the -*stathir* farms named after women proved to be 17 per cent of those named after men, but in other sections, only about 9 per cent.

When the first census was taken in Iceland, in 1703, the country was divided into 164 hreppar (parishes). A century and a half later, when Jón Jónsson published his register of farms, the distribution of these parishes was almost unchanged, and they numbered 167. Two of these are called Saurbær, and altogether nineteen Saurbær farms are known in Iceland. It may attract particular attention that on the site of five of these, old churches had been located, and a chapel on a sixth. In addition, most of these Saurbær farms were quite close to old church sites, and never on the outskirts of settlements. This distinctive feature gives a clear indication as to their origin, since we know that at the beginning of conversion churches were always built near, or on the site of, heathen sanctuaries.

Now, as luck would have it, there is a fairly precise description in the Book of Settlements of the first settlement in both the parishes known as having *saur*- farms. The landtaking in this portion of the Dales District is described as follows:[3]

> Steinólf the Short, the son of the *hersir* Hrólf of Agthir, took land from the Klofa Stones to Grjótvallarmúli, and dwelled in Fagradale at Steinólfshjalli. He entered into the mountains, and inside of them he saw a large valley all overgrown with woods. He detected a clearing in that valley. There he had his farmhouse built and called it Saurbær, because there was much boggy

[3] *Ldn.* § 165.

ground, and he gave the same name to the entire valley. The place where the farm stood is now called Torfness. Steinólf married Eirnýja, the daughter of Thithrandi . . . Arndís the Wealthy was their daughter. . . . *Three swine got away from Steinólf. They were found two years later in Swinedale, and there were then thirty swine.*

The accounts touching on the Saurbær Parish in the Eyjafjord District are likewise noteworthy. Helgi the Lean, the son-in-law of *hersir* Ketil Flatnose, at first took possession of the entire Eyjafjarthardale. Arriving there,

> *he put two swine on land, a boar called Solvi, and a young sow.* Three years later *they were found in Solvadale, and then there were* 70 *swine altogether.* . . . Helgi gave Authun rotin land from Háls up to Villingadale. He lived at Saurbær. Their children were Einar . . . and Vigdís. Helgi gave his son *Hrólf* all the land east of the Eyjafjarthará River from Hvol up the valley, and he lived at Gnúpufell and erected a large temple.[4]

Gnúpufell is close to Saurbær, and so is Solvadale, where the swine increased their kind so that they grew to be a whole herd in three years.

Both tales of swine are cast in the same mold, and they show clear traces of influences from heathen fertility worship. In the Old Icelandic literature we find only three tales of swine of this nature. The third also occurs in the Book of Settlements. Ingimund the Old, who is stated to be of Gautish origin, like Helgi the Lean, took possession of Vatnsdale and lived at Hof in the Ás parish. His grandfather is called Ketil, "a noble *hersir* in Raumsdale in Norway," but Helgi grew up in Hefn with Thórir, the son of Gunnlaug *Hrólfsson.* When Ingimund moved into the Vatnsdale his daughter Thordís was born, and "*there disappeared for him ten swine, which were found the following fall in Svínadale, when they numbered 120. The boar was called Beigath. He jumped into Lake Svínavatn and swam till his cloven feet fell off. He died of exhaustion on Beigathar Knoll.*"[5]

4 *Ldn.* § 265.
5 *Ldn.* § 226.

Ás parish is one of eighteen parishes of our country in which are located Saurbær farms. Thus, all three tales about swine take place in such parishes, though the total number of parishes is 164. Altogether there are fifteen tales about swine in the old literature, all located in Iceland in heathen times, and nine of them occur in parishes with Saurbær farms. We may be absolutely certain that this is not accidental. One of them concerns the grandson of Thordís, the daughter of Ingimund the Old; another, the son of Vigdís, the daughter of Helga, the first mistress of Saurbær in the Eyjafjord District; and the third is transacted on the pavement in front of the farmhouse of Saurbær on Hvalfjarthar Strand. So it would appear as though the closest ties existed in Iceland, during heathen times, between the worship of swine and the *saur-* farms.

Helga in Saurbær was the granddaughter of a *hersir*. She had a daughter with a -*dís* name and a brother who was called Hrólf. Steinólf the Short, who established a farm Saurbær in the Dalar District, was the son of *hersir* Hrólf, and his daughter bore a -*dís* name. Ingimund the Old was a grandson of a *hersir* and was brought up by a man of the line of Hrólf. He also had a daughter who bore a -*dís* name. It is thus not only tales about swine which distinguish the three parishes, together with their Saurbær farms. Here we have to take into account also the appellations *hersir*, *dís*, and *Hrólf*. It behooves us now to consider those Saurbær farms which became the sites of churches. In addition to the Saurbær in the Eyjafjord District, where Helga lived, they are Saurbær on the Hvalfjarthar Strand, Saurbær at Rauthasand, Saurbær at Skjáldbreith, and Saurbær on Kjalarness.

The Hvalfjarthar Strand was occupied by "Kolgrím the Old, the son of *hersir* Hrólf who lived at Ferstikla."[6] Right close by is Saubær, the scene of the tale of the swine. The first one to live at this Saurbær was Hróthgeir the Gentle, the father-in-law of Kolgrím. Rauthasand was taken by a man who had a grandson by the name of Hrólf of Rauthasand. As to Saurbær at Skjáldbreith, that parish was deserted a long time

6 *Ldn.* § 72.

ago, so that one cannot be sure who took possession of that tract. But a short distance away there lived the settler Eyvind karfi. His grandson was called Hrólf. The land around Saurbær on Kjalarness was taken by a son of a *hersir* called Helgi bjóla, the maternal uncle of Helga and of Hrólf at Gnúpufell. From the brothers and sisters of Helga are descended great families of skalds and *dísir*.

We have very clear indications that the Hróth- names had some connection with the culture prevailing on the Saurbær farms. Let us take the list of names in the Book of Settlements and consider how many settlers have Hróth- names or have sons or fathers with such names. They are twenty-five in number, with twenty-seven namesakes. We are informed exactly about the location of all these settlers, so it is easy to discern how the Hróth- names are distributed among the 164 parishes of Iceland. Nine of them are accounted for by the eight Saur- bær parishes, but only eighteen by all the other 146 parishes, i.e., proportionally one-half against one-eighth.

The *Hróth*- names we shall discuss fall into six groups, with the names Hróar and Hróthgeir counted in the same group, because, as Lind states in his excellent book on names, Hróar is derived from Hróthgeir. These are precisely the names, together with Hrólf, which characterize those parishes which have Saurbær farms. We must discuss in a little more detail what is the cause of this remarkable fact. Among the kings of old who bore names with Hróth-, the kinsmen Hróar Hálfdanarson and Hrólf kraki are by far the most famous in lay and legend. Snorri Sturluson says[7] about Hrólf kraki that "he was the noblest of all kings of old, foremost in generosity, bravery, and humility." In Bēowulf, Hróar is the powerful and noble Skjoldung king. It is evident now why in the settlement period the names Hróar-Hróthgeir (Old English Hrōthgār) and Hrólf characterize the Saurbær parishes: The cause lies in the fact that the people who settled in these tracts preserved their age-old family traditions and made much of the Skjoldung kings.

When we consider the lineage of Helga in Saurbær, that is immedi-

7 *Skáldskaparmál*, Chapter 41.

ately apparent. Her ancestry can be traced to the Skjoldung king Ingjald, the son of Fróthi. Helga's brother, Hrólf of Gnúpufell, is the son of Helgi, just like his namesake Hrólf kraki. Hrólf's sons bear the same names as King Ingjald and Bothvar bjarki, the foremost champion of Hrólf kraki. The third brother was called Valthjóf, and that name is analogous to that of Wealtheow, King Hróar's queen in Bēowulf. According to Saxo's History of the Danes, King Hrólf's sister and Bothvar's wife bore the name Ruta, which, as Axel Olrik has shown, is a corruption of the woman's name Hrút.[8] Analogous to it is the man's name Hrút(r). In Iceland it occurs only in that branch of the family descended from Thuríth, the aunt of Helga in Saurbær and Hrólf at Gnúpufell.

Hrólf Helgason at Gnúpufell had one daughter. She lived at Hleithrargarth in Saurbær parish. Two farms in Iceland have that name, one in the landtake of Uni the Dane, the father of Hróar the Tungugothi. The father of Uni, who is stated to be of Swedish extraction, is said to have had landed property on the Danish island of Seeland. Now, when we also note that the three men besides Hróar the Tungugothi, who in the Book of Settlements bear the name Hróar, are all said to have some legendary connection with the race of the Skjoldung kings, one may clearly discern what is the origin of the Icelandic name Hróar. And the same is true with regard to the farm name Hleithrargarth: Thus Icelanders have always called the famous seat of the Skjoldung kings Hleithr. The preservation of Skjoldung legends may thus be said to be among the most distinctive characteristics of the people who established the Saurbær farms in Iceland. Here let us again consult the list of names kept in the Book of Settlements and count those settlers who had mothers or daughters with -*dís* names. There are seventeen men related to eighteen women bearing -*dís* names. Every third -*dís* name occurs in the Saurbær parishes, so that the same proportion obtains between them and the other parishes as before in the case of *Hróar* names. Women with -*dís* names are for the most part stated to be kin to kings, earls,

[8] *The Heroic Legends of Denmark* (1919), Chapter II, no. 4.

and *hersar*, or else were married to men of such lineage. Conforming well with the names of these high-born women with -*dís* names, their lineage is traced through many generations. And although such genealogies in individual cases are worth little, yet they demonstrate unmistakably that at the time of the Settlement -*dís* names were especially common among the foremost chieftainly families which emigrated to Iceland. And that tells its own story.

From the end of the Period of Settlement (*ca.* 930 A.D.), some twenty family heads wielded most power in Iceland. They were called *gothar*, and the core of power of each was the sanctuary. It was owned by the *gothi*, and he himself officiated in it. It was determined that in each Quarter there were to be nine chief sanctuaries, and three in every *thing* (assembly). The domain of the *gothi* who owned such a chief sanctuary was called a *gothorth* (a *gothi's* authority). This term best shows the close connection between the sanctuary and the public religious ceremony. Even though our sources lend no support for the existence of *gothar* or *gothorth* in Norway after the colonization of Iceland, it ought to be evident that in this matter we are not dealing with a purely Icelandic innovation, but rather with an organization which had thrived for a long time among the ancestors of the Icelandic settlers before Scandinavians migrated to Iceland. At the time churches came to be built, these, like the sanctuaries, were the private property of the chieftains. By contrast we see that in Norway, after the conversion, provincial, regional churches were built, and such also for the smaller and smallest divisions of the country. This permits us to draw the conclusion that in Norway the more considerable sanctuaries had, on the whole, not been the hereditary property of the individual chieftainly families, but were rather the collective property of the heathen congregation, and that their members officiated by turn at the public ceremonies. For this reason it is not to be expected that we find memories in Norway of a class of *gothar* or priestesses.

During the heathen period -*dís* names were common in Iceland, and they occur also in the Eddic lays; but in Norway none are found except in the families of those who migrated to Iceland. Lind counts fifteen -*dís* names, with diverse first elements, of Icelandic women in heathen times, but only four among Norwegian women, and these occur much later. Also, the Norwegian -*dís* names of any kind are so rare that one must consider it doubtful whether this group of names ever took root in Norway during the Middle Ages.

The scarcity of -*dís* names in Norway, as compared with the great number of such in Iceland, is an important index of cultural history. It is not by chance that the heathen priestess Freyja was called Vanadís (*dís* of the Vanir gods). The words *dís* and *gythja* designate both a divine feminine being and a priestess. In those families which generation after generation officiated at the public religious ceremonies the occupational title gradually became a baptismal name with the most diverse first elements, as is seen in Iceland in the olden times. It is such -*dís* families which have put their distinctive stamp on those parishes which had *saurbær* farms. Also, it becomes evident that the -*dís* names from the Age of Settlement very often occur in parishes that have *hof*- farms. And this is quite natural: -*hof* farms and *saur*- farms are old sanctuaries. As compared with groups of farms in Iceland with other individual names, proportionally most churches were built on -*hof* and *saur*-farms. Next in order of frequency come the -*fell* farms, as might be expected, because in heathen times people worshipped mountains, as legends and place names show. All the same, churches on *saur*- farms are proportionally by half more numerous than those on -*fell* farms.

As was mentioned above, one of the chief distinctive features of *saurbær* settlements is the great number of -*stathir* farms there named after women. It is the same whether we compare with the number of farmsteads in the census of 1703 or the list of 1847; the result is exactly the same. When we take into account those *saurbær* parishes which had women with -*dís* names, we note that in these parishes every fourth -*stathir* farm is named after a woman. In such parishes the woman -*stathir* farms number 27 per cent, or almost three times more than might be expected before inquiring into the matter. This circumstance can hardly be explained except in one way: It was women who officiated at the religious ceremonies of the Saurbær farms. In other words, *because of the great esteem in which they were held, their dwelling places were bound to be named after them proportionally.*

Skalds and women with -*dís* names are markedly often stated in the old literature to belong to the same families. This is an especially clear characteristic of *hersar* families. This is not the place to mention single instances, nor is that necessary. It can be demonstrated in a much simpler way that there was a connection in heathen times between skaldship and the sanctuaries of the *dísar*, viz., the *saurbær* farms. Skáldatal (Enumeration of Skalds) in the Uppsala version of the Prose Edda[9] now stands us in good stead. We know the birthplaces of the twenty-two skalds there named who flourished in the tenth century and the first part of the eleventh. Nine of them were born or were brought up in Saurbær parishes. In this case the proportion would be one-half as against one-eleventh; that is to say, the skalds from Saurbær parishes prove to be five times more numerous than those from other parishes in the land. This difference is so striking that it makes little difference though it be argued that in heathen times there was an uncommonly dense population around the Saurbær farms. For that matter, it is as clear as daylight that -*stathir* farms named after women, -*dís* names, tales about swine, *Hróth-* names, and skaldic culture are the distinguishing and interrelated characteristics marking the culture of the *saurbær* farms.

It is very significant to find the following story in the Skáldatal: "*Erp lútandi committed a murder in the sanctuary and was condemned to die for it. He composed a* drápa [a longer skaldic poem with a refrain] *about the royal dog Saur and was pardoned for it.*" The dog Saur occurs also in other legendary accounts. King Eystein illráthi (the Evil) is stated to have at one time given the people of Throndheim the choice whether they would prefer to have as king the dog Saur or the thrall Thórir faxi.

---

[9] *Snorra Edda*, ed. Jón Sigurthsson and Finnur Jónsson (Copenhagen, 1880–1887), III, 271.

They chose the dog.[10] Behind Faxi plainly stands a being representing the divinity of fertility. In the year 1854 the image of a god was found in Sætersdale in South Norway which only a short time before had been worshipped by a woman. It was called Faxi, and it had been the custom to anoint this image at Yule with hog lard.[11] The concept of such a Faxi appears also in an Icelandic document from the fourteenth century.[12] In that a certain viking is named Otunfaxi, which probably means "the anointed Faxi." One may then argue that behind the royal dog also there is a memory of a divine being of that name. And this becomes altogether evident when our attention is directed to the account in the Skáldatal. The court skald Erp lútandi murders a man in the sanctuary dedicated to Saur. It is for this reason that he composes his head ransom poem in praise of the dog.

The author of Skáldatal makes out all the court skalds flourishing before the time of Harald Fairhair, with the exception of Starkath the Old, to be the skalds of King Eystein beli. Together with Erp they number ten. In the Hervarar saga King Eystein is called the Evil and is stated to be the son of the Skjoldung king Harald hilditonn. It appears that the legend of the royal dog Saur about which Erp composed his *drápa* has caused the eleven skalds to be made court skalds of King Eystein. This is very typical, since it is clear that the most intimate connection must have existed between Saurbær farms and the flourishing of skaldship among the forebears of the Icelanders. This connection can hardly be explained in any other way than by realizing that at one time Saur was venerated as the god of skaldship.

Thus also is to be understood the case of Óth, the husband of the goddess Freyja.[13] The word Óth signifies skaldship, poetry. According to the statement of Ari Thorgilsson the Wise,[14] a verse about Freyja was composed at the Althing (General Assembly) in the year 999. In it

[10] *Hákonar saga góða*, Chapter 12.
[11] See *Nordisk Kultur*, Vol. XXVI (Copenhagen, 1942), p. 108.
[12] *Thorsteins saga Vikingssonar*, Chapter 20.
[13] *Gylfaginning*, Chapter 34.
[14] *Íslendingabók*, Chapter 7.

the goddess is called a bitch. Still further, one of the popular Icelandic legends[15] deals with a dog supposed to have power over the wealth of its owner. When the dog was killed the owner's wealth vanished. Both the verse and the legend point to influences from an age-old worship of dogs. But by far clearer, however, are the connections in the religious life of our forefathers between Freyja and swine. She is called Vanadís, and her boar, Vaningi. In addition, Freyja has the name Sýr, like the young sow. Indeed, one might imagine that Saur and Sýr were honored as a divine husband and wife, much as Óth and Freyja. The close connection which obtained in heathen times in Iceland between skaldship, worship of swine, and *saur-* farms would point to such a conception.

All the main distinctive features of *saur-* farm culture are exhibited in a remarkable fashion in the Eddic lay Hyndluljóth. Freyja is the paramour of Óth. At the same time, she has the interest of the hero, Óttar the Silly, much at heart. Concerning the reason for her good will, the poet has her say:[16]

> He a high altar made me/of heaped stones—
> all glary have grown/the gathered rocks—
> and reddened anew them/with neats' fresh blood;
> for aye trusted Óttar/the ásynjur [goddesses].

Freyja seeks information concerning Óttar's family tree from Hyndla, "who dwells in a cave." For travelling she rides on a boar and tells Hyndla that two dwarfs, Dáin and Nabbi, have forged her golden-bristled Hildisvíni, which gleams. Hyndla agrees to Freyja's request and traces Óttar's lineage for him. Among other things, she is made to say:[17]

> Thou art, Óttar,/from Innstein sprung;
> but Innstein was born/to Álf the Old. . . .
> Your sire married Móthir/a fair-dight maiden.

[15] See Jón Thorkelsson, *Thjóthsogur og munnmæli* (Reykjavik, Nytt safn), pp. 370–371.
[16] *Hyndluljóth*, stanza 10.
[17] *Ibid.*, stanzas 12 f.

I ween she was hight/*Hlédís the Priestess*. . . .
Of old was Áli/among earth's greatest;
before lived Hálfdan/highest of Skjoldungs. . . .
[He] home led Álmveig,/the most high-born woman—
they issue had/of eighteen sons.
Thence the Skjoldungs,/thence the Skilfings,
thence the Othlings,/thence the Ynglings,
the landholders thence,/the lords's stock thence,
who of most worth are/in the world of men:
*thy sib all these, silly Óttar.*

As may be seen, there is no doubt as to what the poet means with the words: "thy sib all these, silly Óttar." Óttar's is the stock which had its origin from Hálfdan, highest of Skjoldungs. This high-born Hálfdan appears also in Bēowulf, and there is stated to be the grandson of Skjold and the father of King Hróar. There also we hear of the people called *Halfdanes*. Hálfdan is the name of the ancestor of Óttar the Silly. This high-born Hálfdan is analogous to the prehistoric Kings Dan and Gaut. These names are all derived from the names of the peoples.

The Lay of Hyndla reveals clearly where the Halfdanes had their habitat at the beginning of the Viking Age. It is in Norway, especially West Norway. In the poem, branches of the family are referred to which, according to Icelandic tradition, must have lived in Horthaland and taken part in colonizing Iceland. It is also mentioned in an Icelandic source[18] that Skjold was the son of a king from Vors in Horthaland. But no other single district of Norway furnished such a large proportion of settlers in Iceland as did Vors. Ten settlers from there are mentioned, and four Vors farms are known in Iceland. Of the greatest significance, though, is the fact that *holdar* (landholders, yeomen) and *hersar* (barons) should be counted among Hálfdan's offspring. As Edward Bull[19] has shown, *hersar*, as a class of that name, were at that time specifically confined to West Norway. Among Icelandic settlers,

[18] *Flateyarbók* (Christiania, 1860), I, 370–371.
[19] *Scandia*, III (1930).

who mostly came from West Norway, many are said to be the descendants of *hersar*—whether sons or grandsons of such. There are so many instances that they give a clear indication that the main stock of the Icelandic people is the issue of Halfdanes.

From the earliest times Icelanders appear to have been considered in Norway as of yeoman stock, like the descendants of Hálfdan in the Lay of Hyndla. The agreement which King Saint Ólaf drew up with the Icelanders[20] begins with the following words: "Icelanders are to have yeomen's rights in Norway." And the Older Gulathing Laws offer testimony to the same effect. There we read: "Icelanders have the rights of yeomen while on trading journeys until they have resided here for three years and have lived here. Thereafter they are to enjoy such rights as men bear witness they should have. All other foreigners who come to this land shall have farmers' rights unless testimony is offered to the contrary."[21]

The decree about Icelanders' having yeomen's rights in Norway is most remarkable, not least because alodial rights were never adopted in Iceland. There, all freeborn men were equal before the law, in contrast to what was customary in Norway during the Middle Ages. Yeomen's rights of Icelanders in Norway no doubt are an inheritance from their ancestors, the Halfdanes, who formed a superior class in the western shires of Norway before they emigrated to Iceland. Probably following their example, the West Norwegian alodial farmers adopted these rights: The old laws of Norway leave no doubt that yeomen's rights were different, and greater, in those parts from which Icelanders in the main came than in East Norway. There, the term *hǫlth* signified the same as "farmer," and the rights of *holthar* were the same as the right of farmers.

The word *hǫlthr* was preserved in Norwegian legal language for the reason that particular rights were connected with it; but in Icelandic legislation the term was dropped, as might be expected, since equal

---

[20] *Grágás*, § 248.
[21] *Older Gulathings Laws.*

rights obtained among members of the community. Neither was the chieftainly title *hersir* ever used there, which also has its evident and natural reason. In the Book of Settlements, which tells about some four hundred settlers, there is nothing ever said about *gothar* among their forebears nor about *hersar* among themselves or their descendants. From this we may conclude that the term *gothi* superseded the *hersir* title, or, in other words, did away with it among the Halfdanes who settled Iceland. Such a turn of events has its own history. And now the *-dís* names, the Saurbær culture, and Hyndluljóth afford us help in explaining this phenomenon.

Óttar the Silly, the grandson of the priestess Hlédís, figures in this lay as the representative of the Halfdanes. "Ay believed Óttar in the ásynjur," as the poem has it. The Swine goddess Freyja with her golden-bristled Hildisvíni is the divinity he worships. For her he raises a high altar. But times change, and people with them. In the tumult of the Viking Age, big, burly Thór, armed with the hammer Mjolnir, gradually pushes Freyja aside in the religious life of our forefathers. The name-giving of that period shows that unmistakably. *Thór-* now becomes by far the most common first element in the *-dís* names of Iceland. The menfolk of the *hersar* families, who formerly, so to say, had the secular leadership of the people in their hands, now in great part take over also the performance of the public religious ceremonies from the priestesses. At the same time, the honorific title of *hersir* is changed to *gothi*. This change took place mainly in the generations *during which Iceland was being settled, before and right after 900 A.D.*

There has been much controversy concerning the age of Hyndlu-ljóth, and it will hardly ever be determined with any certainty. But this is sure, that the matter of the poem is age-old. Symbolic in this connection is the tradition about the boar Hildisvíni which the dwarfs forged for Freyja. From Bēowulf we may gather what kind of boar that was. The poet says that weaponsmiths in the olden times adorned helmets with the images of boars, so that they could stand both sword blows and fire. These boar images must have been of gold, and either set in an ornamental border which ringed the helmet, or else fastened above the crown of the helmet. Finds of antiquities have confirmed accounts of boar images on helmets. None of these antiquities is likely to be later than from the seventh century. The poem of Bēowulf might with justice be named after the Skjoldungs, who were descended from the high-born Hálfdan, like Óttar the Silly. And now it so happens that no hero of old is so surrounded by tales of swine as is Hrólf kraki, the nephew of King Hróar, the son of Hálfdan. When Hrólf visits King Athils in Uppsala, he is fiercely attacked by a boar which Athils had sacrificed. Queen Yrsa gives her son Hrólf the ring Svíagrís (Pig of the Swedes), and on his flight from Uppsala he casts this ring down before King Athils, who is pursuing him. And when Athils bends down to pick up the ring, Hrólf exclaims: "Now I made stoop like a pig him who is mightiest among the Swedes." Finally, a fearful boar decides the outcome of the battle Queen Skuld brought on. "There flies an arrow from each of his bristles, and he kills the warriors of Hrólf in heaps in a monstrous fashion." All these instances are from the saga of Hrólf kraki.

Snorri Sturluson also tells a remarkable story about swine:[22] Aided by the champions of Hrólf kraki, King Athils felled Áli of Uppland and "took from his dead body the helmet Hildisvín and his horse called Raven. Thereupon the berserkers of King Hrólf kraki demanded their pay, . . . and besides they demanded to bring Hrólf kraki the valuables they chose for him, which were the helmet Hildigolt and the byrnie Finnsleif, against neither of which iron was effective, and also the gold ring called Svíagrís which had been in the possession of Athils' forebears."

Now we can see that it is not by chance that tales about swine and the *Hróth-* names Hróar, Hróthgeir, Hrólf all agree as being distinctive features of the *saurbær* parishes. Both, like skaldship, are inherited from the *-dís* women of the race of Hálfdan who officiated at the religious ceremonies in *Saurbær* farms. And with profound wonder we observe

[22] *Skáldskaparmál*, Chapter 41.

that the leading boars of the swine herds of Ingimund the Old and Helgi the Lean are honored with the names of famous heroes of yore from the time when it was customary for men to wear "battle swine" on their helmets and ring swords by their sides. They were named Beigath and Solvi. Beigath was one of Hrólf's champions who would rob King Athils of Hildisvín and Svíagrís. An earl from Jutland by the name of Solvi is supposed to have felled King Eystein, the son of Athils, and to have made himself king of the Swedes.[23] I have no doubt that there is a connection between the naming of these heroes and of the sacred boars, who were the symbol of fertility. After Ingimund found his herd of swine and the leading boar Beigath, he felt happy in Vatnsdale.

In his treatise on helmets and swords in Bēowulf,[24] Knut Stjerna demonstrated the remarkable agreement which exists between the statements of the poem concerning the armament of men and certain kinds of helmets and swords which were the fashion with East Scandinavian chieftains of the sixth century, as evidenced by the antiquities. Besides ornamental helmets with the images of boars atop them and representations of such on the metal borders around them, there is frequent mention in the poem of the characteristic ring swords. They are so named from a ring attached to the upper hilt. Very probably this ring symbolized the sun and was a sacred token like the altar ring of the Icelandic *gothar*, three centuries later. On this kind of ring men swore sacred oaths. Toward the end of the seventh century men ceased to fasten rings to sword hilts, and exactly about the same time the use of ornamental helmets came to an end in the North. But the memory of these chieftainly treasures is preserved in Norse stories and poems which, however, are of a much later time than Bēowulf. Ring swords are mentioned in the Lays of Helgi Hjorvarthsson and of Sigurth Fáfnisbani, ornamental helmets in the Lay of Atli, King of the Huns, and in

[23] *Ynglinga saga*, Chapter 31.
[24] *Essays on Questions Connected with the Old English Poem of Bēowulf* (1912), Chapter 1.

the Lay of Hloth. Thorbjorn hornklofi, in his Lay of Harald, also mentions "graven helmets." But, as Håkon Shetelig reminds us in his History of Norway,[25] "the poetic vocabulary harks back to times older than the poet's." It is clear that in the sixth and seventh centuries there was a close association between the custom of wearing helmets adorned with images and having rings attached to sword hilts. In Bēowulf both are seen at the same time, and the custom is plainly linked with the religious ideas of those who follow it. Ring swords and image-adorned helmets have been found in the same grave, and on a bronze plate from the early seventh century unearthed on Öland there is the representation of a man with a ring sword in his hand and a helmet with the image of a boar on his head. These antiquities suggested to me the thought that it might be worth while to find out in what sorts of legendary Norse traditional accounts of ring swords and ornamental helmets are encountered.

On investigating this, a peculiar fact was brought out: King Helgi Hjorvarthsson has a ring sword, and his brother Hethin "lays his hands" on the *sonargolt* (the sacrificial boar) and makes a vow. Sigurth Fáfnisbani has a ring sword, and his wife drinks a *sonardreyra* (the sacrificial boar's blood), while her brothers wear ornamental helmets. Hloth has such a helmet, and his father, a *sonargolt*. King Athils possesses the helmet "Hildisvín" (Battle Swine), and his forebear performs a *sonarblót* (sacrifice of the boar). Here there are, then, on the one hand, ring swords and ornamental helmets which fit in with the descriptions in Bēowulf of the armament of East Scandinavian chieftains of the sixth and seventh centuries; on the other hand, we have four tales about swine which show the same characteristic features which distinguish them from all other tales about swine in literature, and that is the first element of the words *sonarblót*, *sonardreyri*, and *sonargolt*. In the opinion of Eduard Sievers,[26] the words *sonardreyri* and *sonarblót* have an erroneous form in Icelandic writings, and should more correctly be

[25] *Det norske folks liv og historie* (Oslo, 1930), p. 333.
[26] *Paul und Braune Beiträge*, XVI (1892), 540 ff.

*sonargoltardreyri* and *sonargoltarblót*. About this there can be no doubt.

The clearest and chief characteristics of *saurbær* culture are the worship of swine and the art of skaldship. It stands to reason that both were associated among the Halfdanes for many years before Iceland was colonized. At the same time, we may infer from the *sonar-* words that the worship of sacrificial boars and the custom of wearing ring swords and helmets ornamented with figures followed the same course. Nor are the connections between these customs and the Old English and Norse poetic language less clear. Kennings are characteristic of both Anglo-Saxon and Old Norse poems. Helmets occur extremely frequently in kennings. Even God is called the "helmet of heaven" in Bēowulf, and in our own ancient poetry we find the helmet in exceedingly many compounds which may be interpreted as kennings. The cause for this certainly lies in the old custom of having sacred symbols like the Hildisvíni of Freyja on the helmets. The realistic and exact choice of words which the poets use for the distinctive characteristics of ornamental helmets and ring swords shows that Norse skaldship in the olden times thrived among people who wore these precious possessions.

The chief concern of Bēowulf derives from East Scandinavian sources. The same is true of the Ynglingatal and the heroic lays of the Edda. Those who first employed this subject matter in poetic production of the North drew especially on traditions which had their locus on the islands and shore lands of the Baltic, and also on legends of the "southern ways", where the Goths and Huns had fared. On the other hand, the Norse settlements along the Atlantic seaboard appear to lie entirely beyond the ken of these poets. No traditions and very few place names from there occur in the old poems. However, it was the descendants of the Halfdanes in Iceland who preserved this cultural inheritance and steadily added to it. At the same time, we must remember that at the time when epics began to flourish in the Northlands one becomes aware of a great difference in the characteristics of antiquities from West and East Scandinavian settlements. Different cultural streams from the southeast and the south exert their influence on the North. It is the resulting so-called Vendel or Mainland style which sets its stamp on the fashion of ornaments and weapons of East Scandinavian chieftains. It is stated to bear evident marks of influence from Byzantium and Italy and to have come to the North by way of South Germany. Now we know with certainty of a Scandinavian people who at the time of the Great Migrations had close connections with Byzantium and Italy. They were the Herúli, who, in the opinion of Otto von Friesen and Sophus Bugge,[27] brought the runes to the Northlands. According to Prokopios,[28] bodies of Herúli from the south settled in the neighborhood of the Gauts at the beginning of the sixth century. We are not informed in ancient sources, whether Greek or Roman, of any other migration of a southern tribe to the north.

Whenever the Vendel style and the origin of epic poetry in the North are discussed, the mind is bound to turn to the Herúli. In the third century they, together with the Goths, migrated to southern Russia, settling by the Sea of Azov, to the east of the Gothic settlements. There, according to Snorri Sturluson, the Æsir and the Vanir gods are supposed to have dwelled before they brought skaldship to the Northlands, establishing themselves first on Funen, then in the Swedish Uppland where lie the towns of Uppsala, Sigtúna, and Vendel, famous of old. From Vendel in Uppland the southern style of ornaments derives its name.

About the middle of the fourth century the Herúli submitted to the leadership of Ermanarík, the powerful king of the Ostrogoths, who in the Eddic lays and the Volsunga saga is called Jormunrek. When, somewhat later, the Huns irrupted into the Black Sea lands, the Ostrogoths had to bow to their power, and the same fate overtook the Herúli. Then, on the ruins of the great empire of Atli, the king of the Huns, there arose, in the latter part of the fifth century, a powerful kingdom of the Herúli in eastern Hungary. The Herúli took an import-

[27] See p. 121, notes 31 and 32.
[28] *Historikon* vi. 14. 1; 15. 1; 15. 4.

ant part in the expedition of Odovacer to Italy (476), when the West Roman Empire came to an end and, as a reward, received land there in Italy. Scarcely a generation later the Langobards overthrew their dominion and slew their king, Hrólf. It was then that some Herúli departed and migrated to the North under the guidance of chieftains of the royal race, whereas others sought the mercy of the East Roman emperor and were permitted to settle in his dominions. Thousands of them entered the service of the emperors of Byzantium during the sixth century. There is reliable evidence that during this time contact was maintained between the North and South Herúli. It is at this time that one observes the arrival in the North of the Vendel style with its images of boars.

The theory Elias Wessén has set forth[29] that the Skjoldungs were Herúli will hardly be disproved. And N. C. Lukman recently adduced strong arguments[30] that Hrólf kraki is the same person as the king of the Herúli of that name who was slain by the Langobards. Among the descendants of the Herúli who migrated to the North at the end of the fifth century, the memory of King Hrólf was preserved in legend and song. In their eyes he becomes "the noblest of all the kings of old," as Snorri Sturluson expresses himself; whereas Jormunrek and Atli, the king of the Huns, are given a rather poor character, as might be expected. It is a matter of course that the Herúli, who came from the southlands, were far more advanced in all cultural matters than those tribes who had remained in the North. Hence it is but reasonable to suppose that it was the chieftains of the Herúli who maintained skaldic culture in the North before Iceland was settled, and that they there persisted in the leadership which is so evident in the *saur-* farm culture, and later, in that flourishing literary output to which there is nothing comparable in the Middle Ages among Germanic nations. The old Icelandic chieftainly class who had the leadership in cultural matters in their hands was descended not only from the Herúli but had blended with the Danes.

[29] *De nordiska folkstammarna i Bēowulf* (Stockholm, 1927), Chapter 2.
[30] *Skjoldunge und Skilfinge* (Copenhagen, 1943), pp. 125–145.

Hence the name *Halfdanes* and the idea of the father of the race being *Hálfdan*, the highest of the Skjoldungs. Hence also the name "the Danish Tongue" as signifying "our language." Thus did our forefathers call their mother tongue.

# Addenda

The following footnotes should be added:

On page 47, at the end of line 2: *Snorra Edda*, III, 271. For the source and implications of this legend, see Lily Weiser-Aall, *Maal og Minne* (1933), 134 ff.

On page 57, in the first line, after "(Sure Giver)": On the etymology of the name of this field and its relation to the cult of Frey, see Anne Holtsmark, *Maal og Minne* (1933), 111 ff.

On p. 107, ninth line, after "bore this surname": *Ldn.* § 264.

On page 116, in the first line, after "worshippers of the *dísir*": *Op. cit.*, Chapter 15.

# Index

Adam of Bremen, 57, 74
*Ágrip af Noregskonunga sogum*, 101
Alfred the Great, 66
Alodial laws, viii, 6 f., 10 f., 18, 159
Antiquities, ix, 83 ff., 89 ff., 98 ff.,
106 f., 134–135, 141, 143, 161, 164 f.;
*see also* Chapes, Fibulas, Figurines,
Helmets, Images, Miniatures, Saddle
rings, Swords
-*ar* names, 76, 80 ff.
Archaeological Society (Icelandic), 38
Ari the Learned, 3 f., 14 f., 19, 94,
156
Arnald Thorvaldsson, 88
Arndís the Wealthy, 33
Ása-Óthin, 61
Athils, King, 131 f., 134, 138 f., 144,
161 ff.
Atli, King, 142, 165 f.
Auth the Deep-Minded, 32 f., 94 f.,
105, 108, 116

Bandamanna saga, 97
Bēowulf, 114, 124, 126, 134 ff., 138,
140, 151 f., 158, 160 ff.
Bjarnar saga, 27
Boar, home-fed, 49 ff., 122, 139; *see
also* Swine worship
Book of Icelanders (*Íslendingabók*), 3
Book of Settlements (*Landnámabók*),
4 ff., 8, 17, 31, 48, 51 ff., 62 ff., 69 f.,
78 ff., 87, 92, 95 ff., 100, 103, 107 f.,
116 f., 123, 125, 148 f., 151 f., 160;

Hauk Erlendsson version, 31, 128;
Hauksbók version, 63 ff., 73, 105,
111, 129; Sturlubók version, 127
Brandkrossa *tháttr*, 29, 75, 98
British Islands, 4, 13, 66, 68
Bugge, Alexander, 6, 126
Bugge, Sophus, 121, 141, 165
Bull, Edward, 158
Burial customs, viii, 8–10, 50 f., 146
Byzantium, 141 f., 165 f.

Canute the Powerful, 15
Celtic influence, 4, 19, 66, 102, 128,
130, 135
Chapes, 85, 89 f., 92 ff., 104, 109 f.
Christian Laws, 78
Christianity, 36, 49, 95
Churches, 48, 64, 91, 148, 150, 153 f.
Clubs, 68, 82, 133
*Collections for the History of Iceland*, 37,
147
Congress of Scandinavists, vii
Court poets, 23 f., 26, 28–29, 59–60

Dag, King, 138
Danish Tongue, 11, 167
*Daunitar*, 13 f.
-*dís* names, 117–120, 150, 152 ff., 160 f.
*Dísir* worship, 115 f.
Droplaugarsona saga, 26 f., 69 ff., 73,
77, 86, 98
Dudo, 110 f., 117

169

East Scandinavians, 61 ff., 68 ff., 76 ff., 89 f., 93, 95, 99 ff., 110 ff., 117, 128, 130 f., 140 f., 162, 164 f.

Eastland (of Iceland), 25 f., 29–30, 37 ff., 62 ff., 85 ff.

Eastland sagas, 26 f., 31, 53

Eddic lays, 40, 114 ff., 136, 140, 142 ff., 153, 157, 164 f.

Egils saga, 26 f., 68

Einhard, Annals of, 12, 113

England, 13, 114

Erp lútandi, 46, 155 f.

Esphœlinga saga, 97

Eyrbyggja saga, 42, 45, 52, 58, 94, 96

Eyvind the Easterner, 65 f., 99 ff., 106 f., 125, 129 ff.

Farms, -*church*, 48; -*fell*, 48, 154; *hof*-, 48, 154; -*holt*, 48, 77–82; -*lund*, 64, 79; register of churches, 37, 77, 118, 147 f.; *saur*-, 47–49, 51, 58–60, 99, 117 ff., 122 ff., 128, 139, 148 ff., 154 ff., 161, 166; -*stathir*, 36–40, 58–59, 72, 77, 119, 124, 146 ff., 154 f.; with women's names, 35

*Farms and Fanes of Ancient Norway*, 146

Faxi, 155 f.

Fertility worship, 41, 49, 51, 56 ff., 60 f., 64, 73, 76, 83, 85, 94, 99, 119, 134, 149, 156; *see also* Frey, Freyja

Fibulas, 84 f., 88 f., 93, 104

Figurines, 83 ff., 89 f., 104

Fjorleif, 29 f., 34

Flóamanna saga, 49 ff.

*Fornaldarsogur Northrlanda*, 112, 116, 131

*Fornvennan*, 51

Fóstbrœthra saga, 27, 68, 97

Frey, viii, ix, 41 f., 44 ff., 50 f., 54, 57 f., 73 ff., 79, 83 f., 88 ff., 93 ff., 99, 133, 137 f.

Freyja, viii, 35, 41 f., 46, 51, 54, 57 f., 115 f., 119, 132 f., 154, 156 f., 160, 164

Friesen, Otto von, 121, 141, 165

Funen, 143 f., 165

Garthar, 5, 129

"Gaut" names, 103–107

Gautland, 4 f., 77, 79, 83, 89, 93, 121, 125, 131

Geirason, Glúm, 24 f., 28, 34, 59, 62, 64 ff., 89

Geiri, 65 f.

Genealogies, 72 ff., 107 ff., 124

Germany, 13, 141, 165

Gísla saga, 27, 45, 57, 92, 94, 96

Gissur Ísleifsson, Bishop, 25

*Glymdrápa*, 16

Gnúpa-Barth, 63 ff., 89

*Gothar*, viii, 7, 10 f., 153, 160, 162

Graut-Atli, 69 ff., 86 f.

Grettis saga, 27, 97, 106

Grím Droplaugarson, 24, 34, 62, 69 ff.

*Gulathing Laws*, 78, 159

*Gunnar Thithrándabani, saga of*, 98

Gunnlaugs saga, 27

Guta saga, 78

Guthmundsson, Barthi, vii ff.

Guthmundsson, Teresía, x

Guthröth Rognvaldsson, King, 12 ff., 100 f.

Hafr-Bjorn, 95 f.

Hafrsfjord, Battle in the, vii, 15, 66 f., 101

Hákon the Good, King, 18

Hálfdan, 124, 128 f., 132, 145, 158, 161, 167

Halfdanes, 158 ff., 164, 167

Hálfs saga, 112 ff.

Hallfrethar saga, 27

Hallstein of Hofthi, 62 f., 89

Hálogaland, 19, 33

Harald Fairhair, King, vii, 3, 12, 15 f., 18 f., 66 ff., 79, 101, 111, 129, 138, 156
Harald Gormsson, King, 15
Hárek Gundrötharson, King, 12 ff.
Harthar saga, 28, 52, 58
Harvest festivals, 41, 50
Hávarthar saga, 27, 97
Hebrides, the, 62, 100, 108, 129
Heithnarey Island, 41, 47
Heithrík, King, 137
Helga, 122, 125, 150 ff.
Helgi Ásbjarnarson, 24, 62, 73 ff., 79, 86
Helgi the Lean, 4, 25, 29, 31, 51 ff., 62 f., 77, 89 f., 122, 129, 139, 149, 162
Helmets, 131, 134 ff., 143, 145, 160 ff.
*Hersar*, 10, 32 ff., 150 f., 153, 155, 158 ff.
Herúli, vii, ix, 121, 141 f., 165 f.
Hervarar saga, 127, 137
Hethin, 136, 138, 163
Hildisvín, 131 ff., 138 f., 157, 160 ff.
*Historia Norvegiae*, 16
History of Norway, 135, 163
History of Old Norse Literature, 23
History of the Danes, 88, 152
*Holdar*, 158 f.
Hornklofi, Thorbjorn, 16, 66 ff., 71, 82, 101, 111, 135, 138, 163
Horthaland, 17, 113 ff., 158
"How Norway Was Settled," 69 ff.
Hrafnkel Freysgothi, 51, 73 ff., 90
Hrafnkel saga, 26, 76, 86 f., 98
Hrólf kraki, King, 125, 134, 151 f., 161 f., 166
Hrólf kraki, saga of, 128, 131 f., 161
*Hróth*-names, 122–126, 149 ff., 155, 161
*Hyndluljóth*, 157, 160

Images, 79, 83 ff., 93, 156
Ingimund the Old, 52 ff., 63 ff., 70 ff., 74, 76, 78 f., 83 f., 89 f., 93, 101, 103 f., 139, 149 f., 162

Ingjald, King, 124 f., 152
Ingólf Arnarson, 3
Ingunn, 34
Ireland, 13 ff., 65, 100 f., 127, 129 f.
*Íslendingabók*, 3
Italy, 141, 165 f.

Járngerth, 29
Jónsson, Finnur, 23 ff., 27, 37, 62, 64 f., 147
Jónsson, Jón, 37, 77, 147 f.
Jormunrek, King, 142, 165 f.
Jutland, ix, 9, 139

Kålund, P. E. K., 37, 41
Katla, 52 f.
Kennings, 140, 164
Ketil Flatnose, 29, 108, 129, 149
Ketil thrym, 69 ff., 86 f.
Kjalleklings, the, 42 ff.
Kjarval, King, 125, 129 f.
Kormáks saga, 27, 91, 97
Kylfingaland, 101

*Landnámabók, see* Book of Settlements
Langobards, the, 139, 142, 166
Lárusson, Ólaf, 48
Laxdœla saga, 79, 96, 98, 117, 125
Lay of Atli, 135, 162
Lay of Guthrún, 137, 144
Lay of Harald, 16, 66 f., 135, 163
Lay of Helgi Hjorvarthsson, 135, 162
Lay of Hloth, 135, 137, 163
Lay of Hyndla, 114 ff., 124, 132, 157 ff.
Lay of Sigurth Fáfnisbani, 135, 162
Lind, E. H., 70 f., 117, 124, 151, 154
Ljósvetninga saga, 26, 52, 97 f.
Ljót, 32
Lochlannar, 13 ff.
Lukman, N. C., 166

Magic, 30 ff., 35, 52

Mardoll, 29
Melsteth, Bogi, 27
Metronymy, 27 ff., 35, 81, 116, 120
Migration of Nations, 99, 121, 141, 145
Miniatures, 90
Moer, earls of, 4, 108 ff.

National Collection of Antiquities, 92
Neergaard, C. P., 135
Nerman, Birgir, 76, 80, 144
Njáls saga, 46
Nor, King, 69 ff.
Nordal, Sigurthur, 87, 96
Northland, 25, 27, 37 f.

Occasional poets, 24, 26, 28
Odovacer, 142, 166
Ólaf the White, King, 13 ff., 80, 100 f.
    125, 129
Olrik, Axel, 114, 125, 128, 152
Olsen, Magnus, 39, 44, 93, 146 f.
Orkneys, 6, 108, 111
-orm names, 70 ff.
Óth, 156 f.
Óthin, 35, 120, 126
Óttar the Silly, 114 ff., 157 f., 160

Pjetursson, Stefan, ix
Priestesses, 32, 44, 54, 58, 72–73, 88,
    90 f., 93, 95, 116, 119 f., 153 f., 160
Primogeniture, see Alodial laws
Prokopios, 121, 165
Prudentius of Troyes, Bishop, 13 f.

Ragnar lothbró, 126 f., 130 ff.
Ragnars saga, 47, 127
Reykdœla saga, 26, 65, 92, 97 f., 106
Rings, 92 f., 95, 131 f., 134 f., 139,
    161 f.; see also Swords, ring
Rosén, Helge, 51
Russia, 68, 91, 121, 141 f., 165

Sacrifices, 41 ff., 47, 49 ff., 57 f., 74 f.,
    88 f., 93 ff., 137 f.
Saddle ring, 92 f., 95
Saga Fragment about Kings of Old
    (Sǫgubrot), 126
Sagas, see names of individual sagas
Sagas of the Olden Times in the North-
    lands, 112, 131
Saur-, 41 f., 45 ff., 50; see also Farms,
    Swine worship
Saur, dog, 46, 155 ff.
Saxo Grammaticus, 88, 125, 134, 152
Schück, H., 14
Schütte, Gudmund, 50
Scotland, 15, 100 f., 108, 111
Seeland, 5, 65, 77, 125, 128 f.
Shetelig, Håkon, 17, 84–85, 89, 93, 102,
    109, 129, 135, 142, 163
Shetland Islands, 6
Sievers, Eduard, 139, 163
Sigvat Thórtharson, 11
Skagerak, 12, 14 f., 113
Skálda saga, 111
Skáldatal, 28, 155 f.
Skaldship, 24 ff., 59 ff., 81 f., 90 ff.,
    96 ff., 139, 155 ff., 161, 164; see also
    Court poets, Occasional poets
Skjoldungs, 124 ff., 129, 131, 134,
    151 f., 166 f.
Skroppa, 52, 122
Snorri Sturluson, 18, 35, 61, 108 ff.,
    120 f., 125, 131, 134, 138, 141, 145,
    151, 161, 165 f.
Sonar- words, 138 f., 163 f.
Sorceresses, 31 ff., 52, 57–58, 91 f.
Southland, 25, 37 f.
Speech, 8, 11
Steenstrup, Johannes, 68
Steinólf the Short, 48–49, 51, 53, 122,
    148 ff.
Steinunn the Old, 32
Steinvor, 73, 88, 91

Stjerna, Knut, 135, 143, 162
Storm, Gustav, 15, 68, 101
Suebi, 133 f., 139
Summary of the Sagas about the Kings of Norway, 101
Svarfdaela saga, 53
Sváva, 136, 144
Svein Forkbeard, 15
Sveinsson, Páll, 133
Sverri, King, 78
Svíagris, ring, 131 f., 134, 139, 161
Swine worship, 49–54, 56 ff., 76, 90, 119, 122, 127, 131 ff., 149 f., 157, 160 ff.
Swords, 68, 82, 110, 133; ring, 135 ff., 143 ff., 162 ff.

Tacitus, 133 ff., 139 ff.
Thengil, 62 f.
Thór, viii, 42, 44, 49, 51, 94, 160
Thórir snepil, 62 ff., 89 f., 103 f., 108 f.
Thorkel krafla, 56 f.
Thorkelin, Grímur, 132
Thorskfirthinga saga, 52, 58
Thorsness, 42 ff.
Thorstein Síthu-Hallsson, saga of, 26
Thorstein the Red, 108 ff., 125
Thorstein the White, saga of, 86
Thorsteinsson, Hannes, 38
Thórtharson, Skúli, ix
Thórveig, 91 f.
Throndheim, 16–17, 19
Tjorvi the Scoffer, 62, 76

Úlfljót, 17
Uni the Dane, 65, 76 f., 80, 89, 128, 152
Uppsala, 14, 74, 100, 127, 131, 138, 141, 143, 161, 165

Valla-Ljóts saga, 53, 57, 97
Vápnfirthinga saga, 73, 86
Vápnfjord sagas, 26
Vatnsdæla saga, 50, 53 f., 57 f., 74, 76, 78
Vendel, 141 ff., 165 f.
Víga-Glúms saga, 26 f., 53 f., 74 f., 96 ff., 115
Vigfússon, Guthbrandur, 41 f., 46, 58
Volsunga saga, 142, 165
Vries, Jan de, 130

War Alarum *drápa*, 16
Weddings, 53, 57
Wessén, Elias, 106, 166
West Fold, 12 f., 16, 67
Westland, 25 ff., 37 ff.
Wīdsīth, 124, 134
Witch-Manga, 45
Women, viii, 27 ff., 58 f., 61, 146 ff., 154 f.

Yeoman's rights, 159
*Ynglingatal*, 16, 66, 100, 140, 144 f., 164
Yule customs, 136 f., 156

Zimmer, 14